Corporate Storytelling
Planning and Creating Internal Communications

Grendel Press
Loveland, Colorado

GRENDEL
P R E S S

Corporate Storytelling

Planning and Creating Internal Communications

Lecia Vonne Wood

Grendel Press
2002

About the Author

Wood has more than 15 years business experience as an editor and writer and has worked with both small businesses and Fortune 500 companies. She holds a Master's of Business Administration in Global Management.

The ABCs of Business: **Corporate Storytelling — Planning and Creating Internal Communications.** Copyright 2002 by Lecia Vonne Wood. Printed and bound in the United States of America. All rights reserved. No part of this book may be reproduced in any form or by any electronic or mechanical means including information storage and retrieval systems without permission in writing from the publisher, except by a reviewer, who may quote brief passages in a review. Published by Grendel Press, P.O. Box 238, Loveland, CO 80539. First edition.

For information about products from Grendel Press, please call toll-free 1-866-GRENDEL or visit www.grendelpress.com.

ISBN: 0-9714988-1-4
Library of Congress Control Number: 2001098392

Editor: William Rodarmor

Cover design by Erik Watada

Contents

Contents

Acknowledgments

This book is truly the outcome of a group effort undertaken by a squadron of dedicated, thoughtful and generous people. Publisher Sally Slack, who had the incredible faith to start a new publishing venture and include me in it. Editor William Rodarmor, who has patiently given encouragement and oh-so-wise suggestions to improve this text. My sister, Chris Wood, who has entertained my beloved four-year-old daughter weekend after weekend so that she could play and have fun even while I met looming deadlines. And my colleagues, employers and clients over the last sixteen years, who have shared their expertise and vision for best practices in communications.

On a personal note, I'd like very much to hear about your experiences in creating employee communications. If this book helped you, that would be great to know. If you'd like to see it include other types of information, that would also be great to know.

If you have questions beyond what we covered here, contact me directly at lecia@windhorsecomm.com or visit www.windhorsecomm.com.

To Lily, princess of her flower patch,
Peter Pan of the stairs,
and brave cohort of Scooby-Doo!

Preface

When Lecia asked me to write a few comments as a preface for her first book on communications, I was on one hand delighted and on the other hand hesitant as I wondered how could I be succinct on this subject? There's so much I could say about communications in the workplace and what works . . . and what doesn't. But then, that's the continuous challenge in communications — how to speak concisely and clearly! The other challenge is that almost everyone seems to think they're experts when it comes to communicating. Even people with no real knowledge about writing, speaking, educating, or communicating are nevertheless full of opinions about how to do it, what to say, and how to say it.

The good news is that this book is written by someone who not only has that knowledge but also has put it to work in complex and dynamic business conditions.

In my role as a manager at IBM responsible for worldwide education and communications on a complex, enterprise project, one of my recurring challenges is to communicate project outcomes to a wide range of people. Because my job requires that I implement concrete deliverables, I needed a communications expert who could both create and produce what's needed. I found that person in Lecia, and the principles she outlines in this book are principles that we've used and learned from firsthand.

Relationship between client and producer

Lecia and I work together as producer and client, respectively. As the client, I identify the overall needs and direction for delivering the communications, which Lecia then drives to production. The relationship we have drives the process we use and, ultimately, the actual deliverables and their quality. As the client, my job is to understand

and prioritize the information needs, the internal issues, and the players who need to work with us. Lecia's job, then, is to develop the deliverables that are required. One cannot exist without the other. Because the environment is dynamic and complex, the continual give and take of our relationship allows us to be flexible and responsive as the project changes over time.

Credibility of the subject - tell the truth

In a dynamic environment like that of IBM, or any hard-driving organization, if communications don't tell the truth and use the basics of good writing - of who, what, when, where, and why - then they won't work. In our project, we needed communications that addressed somewhat technical subjects. The desire to embellish them to make them more interesting was a strong and understandable push from many quarters. By identifying credible content experts early and "anointing" them to be part of our team, we've been able to stick to a fact-based communications strategy. And because these experts become the owners and reviewers of the communications, they quickly become advocates instead of critics.

What I've learned in working with Lecia is that we accomplish most when we apply fundamental communication principles consistently and creatively. The beauty of this book is that it lays out a blueprint that anyone in any size company and facing any manner of communication challenges can apply immediately with no special training or other resources other than the commitment to communicate accurately, concisely, and clearly. It was created by someone who has "been there and done that." Reading this book will enrich your thinking about communications and give you practical actions to take.

-Carol Burke, Program Director, Worldwide CRM Education, IBM

Introduction

This book exists for two reasons:

1. Because businesses need to improve the way they communicate with employees.

2. Because we can improve that communication now, today, without waiting to solve all the organization's management, leadership, or technical problems.

Sure, organizational and technical factors present long-term challenges to the way companies communicate internally. But other simpler and more accessible factors that we can use now are often overlooked and underused, with the result that employee communications are less clear, less useful, and less effective than they need to be.

This book contains guidance to help ensure that the communications you or your teammates put together meet the most basic criteria for success: accuracy, relevancy, and timeliness for the recipients. By focusing on creating employee communications that really benefit employees, you will also further the objectives of your unit, division, or company.

Corporate Communication Is an Oxymoron!

People communicate, not corporations. At its heart, communication is a grassroots activity. It's about understanding, one person at a time, what is happening in our world. It's about sharing experiences and hopes for the future. It's about how we respond as a community to tragedy or loss. And it's about working together to accomplish the daily tasks of the workplace as well as the larger feats of research, heroism, and profitability.

Communication is about community. In the workplace, our community is built around the products or services we sell or manufacture; around the customers we serve and the industries they're in; around supply and demand, opportunities, efficiencies, using technology and competing; and around the people who do the work to make a product, deliver a service, or satisfy a customer.

Getting down to the basics of communication isn't just a good idea; it's a necessary step if you want to create good memos, presentations, or Web pages. And while it's a simple idea, it's not necessarily easy to do. What it really boils down to are three things: information, engagement, and action. What is it we want fellow employees to know and understand? How will we get this information to them as efficiently and effectively as possible? And what do we want them to do with it once we've gotten it to them?

Face It, Employees Are Customers, Too!

As Bob Pullin, project director for Corsair Studio, a Web design and communications consulting firm in New York City, points out, "Many well-respected brands today carefully craft powerful external communications programs for customers while at the same time harboring dysfunctional internal communications environments that undermine employee effectiveness and morale. Clearly, there are many practical benefits to treating employees more like customers when it comes to communications."

Bill Jensen, president of the The Jensen Group, a New Jersey consulting company that focuses on simplifying work, makes a similar observation. The seven years of research behind his recent book, *Changing How We Work: The New Competitive Advantage in a World of More, Better, Faster,* found that "how we communicate" is the third most common factor that makes work "more complex, frustrating, and inefficient than it needs to be." Research participants included Fortune 250 companies as well as a sampling of small, mid-, and large-sized firms.

Employees today are bombarded by e-mails and phone calls, and yet most still complain that finding the right piece of information at the right time remains a challenge. From the lonely entrepreneur to project and team leaders juggling resources and requirements to CEOs armed with teams of corporate communicators, the task of mobilizing and informing a workforce is vital, yet hard to do well. Perhaps we can reduce complexity and improve the flow of information within the company by taking a simpler and more consistent approach to employee communications.

Five Common Reasons
Business Communications Often Fail

1. Communication is a human, mutable, dynamic exchange between people.

As a human activity, it is subjective and highly dependent on shared references. In global organizations, communicating across language and cultural barriers can be full of difficulty and surprises. Even within the same culture, communication is subject to regional, ethnic, gender, personal, and professional biases.

2. Businesses often implement communications programs without the necessary thought or resources.

Because communication is something human beings do every day, a common perception within organizations is that anyone can do it. And yes, anyone can do it. Just as anyone can put the initials CEO behind his or her name and open up a company. But just as a business has greater chances of success with some strategy and planning behind it, so a communications program has better chances of success when it is based on a solid foundation that includes clear objectives and a realistic messaging strategy. Precisely because communications are so easy to do, they are often implemented carelessly.

3. Communication takes time and repetition.

It takes discussion and give and take. Few, if any, of our business models today encourage employees to use their time this way. Most business models expect time to be used to generate a measurable return such as revenue, customer face time, call time, and so on. The impact of communication efforts on these returns is hard to measure.

An employee might, after several communications events, truly understand and be galvanized by their company's new mission but still fail to beat quota because of other factors. Is this a failure of the organization's communications program? The reverse can also be true. Perhaps the company experiences a stellar quarter with no significant investment in strategic internal communications. So the absence of communications appears not to matter. There is no way to know if performance might have been even better had there been a rallying, actionable communications plan to support the new business program.

Since few business models really accommodate give and take, town hall meetings and similar forums are attended with more skepticism than enthusiasm. The communications model in these environments is typically one-way and vertical — top-down. The intent of the communication is to give information or instructions. The expectation is compliance.

Efforts to establish two-way communication avenues sometimes work but more often fail since the culture and structure of the organization don't support either the activity or the resulting impetus for change and improvement that grass-roots dialogue and exchange elicit. Predominantly one-way communications are less engaging, less compelling, and ultimately less effective.

4. Getting the message to the recipient is often one of the most serious challenges for communicators.

Many companies don't maintain segmentable, or targetable, distribution lists. Many companies can't even compile a single list of their employees with any speed, accuracy, or ease. So while best practices in communications tell us to create targeted messages based on the unique needs of specific groups of people, our ability to get those messages precisely to those people rarely exists. As a result, those asked to communicate with employees are often left in the unpleasant position of having to communicate more or less everything to more or less everyone. This produces a miasma of messages in which nothing stands out with any real clarity, priorities aren't clear, and employees pay no attention to what they receive.

5. Internal communications often miss their mark because they aren't as well constructed as they could be.

This can be caused by some of the factors mentioned previously, but more often it's caused by lack of awareness of basic communications techniques that help ensure clarity, credibility, and understanding. These are techniques anyone can use. They are already used in journalism, film, advertising, and novel writing.

Creating effective communications isn't rocket science!

Suppose someone were to hand you a recipe for creating effective communications? I imagine it would look something like this:

- Take one part common sense.

- Add two parts fact-based observations or directions.

- Mix thoroughly with three parts recipient priorities.

- Season to taste with vision. Avoid sizzle — it will age quickly.

- Bake until consistency is free of jargon, local idiom, unnecessary commas, and long, convoluted sentences.

- Distribute while still warm.

Of course, successful organizational communications depend on many factors, many of which can't and won't be changed overnight. And while visionaries and consultants work to change those factors, my suggestion is that those of us in the trenches of getting work done, sales closed, projects run, and customers served do what we can to ensure our communications are as effective as possible. But what does "effective" mean?

Well, that will depend largely on who you ask. Generally speaking, effective communications are timely, accurate, informative, and compelling (or engaging). From an operational point of view, effective communications describe and elicit desired actions from recipients. From a strategic view, effective communications inspire employees to change, to ascribe to a corporate vision, and to take personal responsibility for the success of the organization. From the recipient's (i.e., the employee's) point of view, the communication should do two things:

1. Deliver immediately usable information that will help me do a better job.

2. Not contribute to the clutter in my in-box.

For most people asked to create and execute an internal communications program, the challenge is to meet everyone's definition of "effective communications." You must accomplish the objective of the sponsor, as that person is answerable for the resources used and has been asked by the organization to meet a certain, specific business objective. Most likely, that business objective has been framed in context of what is best for the organization. So there is probably a collection of operational requirements driving the communications, and they must be met. And finally, everyone will agree, you have to do what's right for the employees, the ultimate recipients and (you hope) beneficiaries of these communications.

Turn Your Priorities Upside-down!

Start with the needs of the employees or whoever is going to receive your communications. What do they need to know? When do they need to know it? And at what level of detail, using what media, with what frequency, and from whom? If you meet the information needs of the target audience, you will fulfill the goals of your project, your sponsoring executive, and your business.

So whether you have managed and generated countless internal communications programs already or if this is the first time you've been asked to quickly create a newsletter for the troops, this book can help you ask good questions, think through your project, and get it out the door successfully.

Use the Tried and True in a New Way!

There's nothing really new here in terms of techniques or writing or planning tips.

What is new is the reminder that these basics are where the real work lies, not in the conceptual realm or in trying to add some sort of sizzle to get readers hooked. The real work has to do with understanding what it is that people need to know and then getting that to them in a usable, engaging way that will help them improve their business. This is the heart of good internal business communications.

Another thing that's new is that this book is intended for project managers and team leaders, many of whom have little or no communications background or related planning or development experience and most of whom are hard-pressed to juggle resources and requirements to move projects forward and close new business. In my experience, these people are intelligent, creative, and resourceful. They appreciate the plight of employees and believe in their organization's ability to deliver value to employees, partners, and customers. This book can give them a vocabulary and a planning and execution framework for the creation of communications to support their efforts. It can also be used as a playbook or process guide by any member of their team asked to actually plan and create communications.

Why bother with this book? Why not just put the team's ideas onto paper and then move forward? My answer is that you will do exactly that. The only difference is that, with this book beside you, you will have a few more techniques, a few more pieces of information, and a few more criteria by which to make communications decisions. And these advantages will help you achieve more with your communications than you might have without. Perhaps you already know everything in this book. Great! Just remember to use that knowledge. Help improve the quality of employee communications!

What's in This Book, Anyway?

The first chapter, *Tools of the Corporate Storyteller* investigates the different types of internal business communications we will explore. We will look at how different types of communication serve different purposes and audiences better than others and introduce the concept of integrating media and deliverables to reinforce messages. The second part of this chapter looks at how principles of good storytelling can be used to strengthen and enliven internal business communications. We'll consider concepts such as the marriage of fact and fiction to build a compelling vision and what it means to show something rather than simply tell it.

In *The Basics*, the book's longest and most important section, we'll review the basics of building good communications plans and messages, fondly known as the Five W's: Who, What, Where, When, and Why. We'll also review a few important writing tips and the basics of approaching a communications project or program strategically.

In *Putting the Basics to Work*, we'll look at the communications needs in two different business scenarios. By the end of the chapter, we will have a documented plan and process for creating and distributing the communications. We'll also know who we need on our team, if anyone, and what qualifications our subject matter experts need to have.

At that point, we'll be ready to start *Fleshing Out the Plan*. By the end of that chapter, we'll have a complete communications plan in hand, including a list of deliverables, audiences and messages, media selection, timeline, and tasks.

With the plan as our foundation, it will be relatively simple go ahead and say *Let's Do It*. In this chapter, we'll look at how the review cycle works, how to solicit, receive, and incorporate feedback from various, often contradictory sources. We'll also look at how core messages can be reused and repackaged in interesting ways to increase frequency. And most importantly, we'll look at how to evaluate the success of your communications and then apply what you learn to continuously improve.

By the End of This Book, You'll Be a Communications Pro!

No one knows everything about employee communications, but everyone has an opinion! So don't be daunted by something that sounds bigger than it is. Stick to the basics, and you will deliver a good product that helps your fellow employees do their jobs more easily.

The tools and principles in this book are proven to be effective — for business as well as entertainment, journalism, and instructional purposes. By applying them in your company or to support your project, you or a member of your team will be able to plan and create internal communications that are strategic in scope and tactical in execution.

No techniques will solve all your communications problems, but those in this book will give you a framework within which to work to ensure you have taken every step you can to generate the most effective messaging possible. With this framework, you will make better decisions regarding communications planning and development resources. You will work around or overcome distribution hurdles. And you will make media and frequency decisions that take into account the activity patterns and messaging preferences of your audiences.

The ability to recognize and manage the many factors that can derail your communications will help you devise ways to avoid or remedy the problem, ways to improve the communications environment in your organization, and finally, will help you set and reach reasonable communications objectives.

So start with the basics, and keep things simple!

Our workplaces today are complex for many reasons. Don't add to that complexity with needlessly complex or unclear or unnecessary communications. Use communications to propel your organization and galvanize your employees to be successful, not just compliant. Contribute with real information at useful intervals using media channels that are easy to access and use.

Tools
of the Corporate Storyteller

Simply put, corporate communications encompasses all the ways in which a company informs, advises, and to some extent, instructs customers, prospects, media, partners, and employees. By "instruct," I mean provide short directions as opposed to formal training or education programs, which require curriculum development.

Communications directed towards customers, prospects, and media are external, while communications directed to employees are internal. Communications to partners can range between the two categories but are more often external in nature. The main difference between internal and external communications is the audience to which the communications are directed. This drives all the other differences, of tone, the level of disclosure, subject matter, media selection, graphics, and product, brand, or company positioning.

For example, customers and media analysts don't need to know about most operational changes, system outages, new benefits packages, or internal incentive programs. However, they do need to know about product or services offerings, terms and conditions, support options, the company's financial performance, and customer testimonials. Partners might need to know about certain incentive programs or operational changes, but they don't need to know about others. But, like customers, they need to know about products and services offerings. And these audiences need to receive this information in contexts that are consistent with the company's external branding and positioning programs, which typically have highly defined graphics and language parameters.

Employees, on the other hand, need to know information about many facets of a company's operations, from changes in the terms of their employment, its rewards and restrictions, expectations and requirements, to changes in how the company does business, including new products or services. And while these topics usually don't need to be conveyed in context of the company's external brand, internal guidelines often apply.

From a communications point of view, content intended for use with employees is more private than that used with customers or partners. For that reason, it is subject to less legal or marketing scrutiny. And internal guidelines are probably fewer in number and less restrictive than those governing externally directed content. This is both good news and bad news. Since internal communications environments are often less structured than external environments, there's a greater potential for inconsistency, poor message construction, and miscommunication.

In this chapter, we'll look at what it means to be a corporate storyteller and what tools you have at your disposal. We'll talk about why your background — which is probably not in writing or storytelling or anything like that — is in fact an asset and not a liability. And we'll talk about five common myths of internal communications.

But What Is a Corporate Story?

Simple. It's the story of how your company, or your unit, or your project goes about its business. How it overcomes obstacles and sets priorities. How its components work together to achieve goals. How changes are implemented. And how employees contribute on a daily, weekly, monthly, or yearly basis. Corporate stories are based on fact, not fiction, and use business and marketplace realities to move the story forward.

One of the greatest challenges is to recognize the value of the story that is right in front of you. Not that it's Pulitzer prize-winning material, but it does matter to someone — even if only your immediate colleagues.

Stories are selective; they aren't archives. Stories are a collection of facts and observations that, when put together, create a narrative that interests and informs the audience.

One of a storyteller's most important jobs is to balance the circumstances of a story so that the trivial plays its role as surely as the monumental. You must select which details to include in the story you're telling and ruthlessly eliminate the rest. The secret is to understand what your audience cares about and what you want or need them to do, which is something we'll discuss in detail in the next chapter.

You don't have to have a degree in English or journalism to tell good corporate stories!

You just need to exercise your powers of observation, reason, and follow-through.

Consider for a moment how storytellers draw us in and engage us so that, years later, we remember a newspaper headline or a pivotal line from a scene in a movie.

They use powers of observation. They advance the story by conveying information that is based on facts and that gives us the ability to become involved, to evaluate whether assertions are true or false, and to draw conclusions about what actions we should take next, as readers or viewers. And storytellers have the ability to recognize and convey the beginning, middle, and end in a story.

In novels or movies, this data leads us on through a plot to its conclusion. At each point along the way we can decide to disengage and withdraw or to continue and find out what will happen next. In business communications, this data tells employees what they need to do quickly, clearly, and easily. Either way, the objective is to foster engagement or relationship by conveying useful or interesting information to the receiver, straight and simple. Storytellers know and remember this.

A Tisket, a Tasket, Check Your Communications Basket!

There are at least as many reasons to create a memo, Web page, or white paper as there are people in a company. And there are practically that many types of internal communications as well, ranging from human resources memos or alerts about changed benefits or employment policies to education announcements, a notice of a management change, changes to the product or services line, system outages, and facilities maintenance alerts.

Executive memos and newsletters may explain why the company is changing its IT structure and moving from one type of technology to another. Some memos ask recipients to do something, others just tell them something. Some Web pages are full of information about an obscure internal project, while others convey new sales training or manufacturing techniques.

Fortunately, there is a limit to the vehicles used to carry this multitude of messages. By "vehicle," I mean the packaging used to hold and then convey the set of messages that make up a communication.

For example, you might have a collection of messages that a sales executive wants to get to his or her sales team. As the communicator, you will decide how to package those messages. Perhaps you can put a few of them into a memo from the executive, and the rest in a presentation attached to the memo. Or you might put those additional messages into a Web article and note the URL in the memo. (See Examples 1 and 2.)

Communication Vehicle	Most Common Uses
Application message lines	Alert application users to system status, planned outages or updates.
	Convey site-specific or application-specific messages
Brochure	Present an internal initiative, change, or expansion in a summary, high-level fashion, and provide contact information for employees to learn more.
Case study	Typically used internally in situations where one part of a company wants to publicize its capabilities in some detail to other parts of the company.
Conferences	Very common internal messaging choice. Formats include face-to-face, telephone, video, and e-meetings. Used when any of the following are critical: 1) executive endorsement, 2) access to executive or specialist to answer questions and give direction and 3) two-way communication.
Handouts	Site-specific announcements such as maintenance-related closures, security precautions, education offerings, etc.
Memos	Used when information to be conveyed does not required two-way interaction. Formats include e-mail, print, executive and cascaded.
Internal news service	Supplement traditional communications. Often targets specific audiences and topics.
Newsletter	Frequently used as a core component on long-term communications efforts. Can be strongest when used in conjunction with Web sites, which house the information to which the newsletter points. Printed newsletters are more frequently used for site-specific information.

Example 1

Tools of the Corporate Storyteller

Either way, you are asking the recipient to read the memo and then take a second action: to access and review either an attachment or a Web page. Other packaging options include newsletters, white papers, case studies, and news items. Another vehicle option would be to deliver those sales messages mentioned earlier in a conference setting, either in person, or by audio or video.

Other packaging and delivery options include leaflets or handouts, posters, public address systems, and message scroll bars at the bottom of applications used by intended recipients. All these vehicles are site-specific and appropriate for delivering messages to employees located in the same facility or location. They would be less effective for employees who work out of home offices, customer sites, or who are on the road as part of their jobs.

Communication Vehicle	Most Common Uses
Posters	A costly communications option that is most useful to audiences who work on site as opposed to mobile workforces.
Presentation	Used to add substance to an e-mail or conference activity. Presentations can be attached to e-mails and downloaded from Web sites to convey info in a graphical format, and reused to extend reach of messages.
Public address system	Used by facilities to convey site-specific information.
Quick reference card	Used to supplement education as well as communication messages. Typically distributed as an e-mail attachment or Web download that can be printed out and referenced for use during the workday.
Talking points	Used by advocates, sponsors, and project executives to ensure team members speak consistently and effectively about a project .
Telephone messages	Used by site management and personnel staff to convey messages to a broad site audience without interrupting workflow.
Web page and site	A continuous and easily updated communication method that gives the ability to publish in a continuous, internally branded fashion. Can address sub-topics in more detail.
White paper	Used internally to articulate strategies, objectives, operational tactics and priorities in detail. Can convey complex messages and support messages that are controversial or conceptually foreign.

Example 2

Five Common Myths About Internal Communications

1. Internal corporate communications are limited to the big guys, with offices in countries all over the world, complex work systems, and revenues of millions of dollars or pounds or rupees.

In fact, internal communications are used by all manner and size of businesses, including dentists' offices, hospitals, local utilities and real estate companies, insurers and agents, IT manufacturers, dog trainers, chiropractors, pharmaceutical companies, supermarkets, financial companies, and YMCAs and colleges. Smaller companies are big users of internal communications — or should be! While it might be easy for smaller companies to make the mistake of thinking everyone knows what's happening just because the organization is small and perhaps close-knit, the truth is more likely quite different. So, rather than play a game of telephone, as most of us probably did in grade school, smaller companies can implement a structured communications program and reduce misunderstanding and wasted time as a result.

It doesn't matter whether you're in a large company or a small one, employees are able to focus more energy on productive and revenue-generating activities when information is easier to find and more consistently communicated. They spend less time trying to find the right piece of data that they need when they need it. They have more time and energy to focus on satisfying customers and delivering the best possible products and services.

2. Internal communications are just memos, and any-body who can write a sentence can write a memo!

Technically, that's true, but before you ship that memo out you might want to ask yourself a few questions. Have I addressed this topic from the point of view of the recipient? Is this format the most useful one I can use for these intended recipients? Is the language as efficient as it can be? And does this communication either help the recipient do something differently and more effectively or does it give them information they can use now, today, to better achieve their business objectives?

3. Tell them everything, just to be sure. But don't say anything definite until it's 100 percent official!

Talk about mixed messages! In large projects that affect many different audiences, there is often such a degree of complexity and uncertainty that isolating the few, truly cogent facts can be quite a challenge. When time is of the essence, that difficulty gets translated into over-communication.

Another common mistake that leads to over-communication is the self-centered idea that everyone in the company, or the division or unit, will find a given topic as fascinating and compelling as its advocates and assignees do. This is rarely the case. The intended recipients of your communication are busy working on their projects or their customers' projects, and they want to know about your project quickly and to exactly the degree that matters to them.

On the other hand, getting messages past those project and middle managers responsible for the new technology deployment or the business process change or the benefits snafu can create the opposite extreme: under-communication. These roles encourage people to wait to communicate until all the wrinkles in a project or a phase of a project are worked out or all the details of a procedural change are understood — which actually means that the topic is sufficiently watered down to not rock the boat.

If you've set solid guidelines for the creation and delivery of communications, you'll find it easier to navigate these choppy waters.

4. Internal communications are boring! Nobody really reads this stuff.

This is often the case, but it doesn't have to be. And it can't be the rule when your company needs to communicate vital information to its employees. You need to ensure that employees get the message and that they understand what it means to them.

To help make communications more engaging, you can resort to all manner of attention-getting devices: from screaming subject lines to cute or dramatic visuals. But the one thing that will get recipients' attention more effectively than anything else is usability: is the information in the message accurate and reliable? Is it relevant to me? Is it something I need to do now, or something that will help me now?

5. Internal corporate communications is limited to those edicts issued by official communications personnel or by the communications team supporting a company's CEO or other senior executive.

Not true! Internal corporate communications are all the pieces that comprise a company's internal dialogue on all sorts of topics, ranging from the earthshaking to the trivial. When taken as a whole, the resulting memos, white papers, Web pages, case studies, presentations, and conference calls tell an organization's story and propel it forward toward marketplace success — or failure.

Internal corporate communications articulate what the company and its parts care about. What it talks about. What it expects its employees to know and understand. How it expects its employees to stay informed and to learn and grow. Internal communications, including the ad hoc, project-driven communications within the corporation, make up the detailed, specific story of the organization and, more importantly, its people.

As with any story, it can be an interesting, compelling story, or it can be tedious, overly detailed, erroneous, and out of date. As a communicator, the choices — and the results — are up to you.

Don't Be a Professional Communicator, Be a Good One!

Many people asked to communicate about something inside a company have no real background in communications, advertising, graphics, or writing. They are just lucky, or unlucky, enough to be in that place at that time.

The good news is that you don't need to have a communications background to be able to plan and generate employee communications. You do need to know a few of the principles and techniques outlined in this book, but we've already talked about that. You need to have access to people who can help you pull together the pieces of information that you'll need — and we'll talk more about that in the *Putting the Basics to Work* chapter.

But there's actually an advantage to coming into a communications role with little to no prior experience: you have a fresh perspective. You won't be tempted to use project or corporate jargon, perhaps. Or you'll be able to reframe the current plan to better address the audience's needs. And you'll be focused on *The Basics*, which is exactly where we're headed next!

But first, take a few minutes to review this chapter's key points. Then take a short quiz.

Key Points

In this chapter, we discussed corporate communications, which consists of two types of communications: external and internal. The most important distinction between these two types of communication is the audience to which each is directed. That one factor then determines the many other factors of a communication, such as tone, subject matter, graphics elements, and distribution methods.

We also discussed what internal corporate stories are made of and who can be a corporate storyteller. Corporate stories are made of the vision and everyday activities of companies and their units or divisions. They are a collection of details that, when strung together, tell a story that motivates or compels employees to act to improve their work patterns or in some other way improve the value that companies offer their customers and partners. Anyone in a company who is observant can select the right details to include in the story and then convey that story to fellow employees. Corporate storytellers don't have special training or highly specialized skills. They can learn the principles of good storytelling and then apply those principles to suit their company's needs. Skills such as follow-through and consistency are also valuable to corporate storytellers.

Different communications vehicles are more suited to certain types of messages and audiences than others. We reviewed a list of the most common vehicles used to communicate with employees and identified those that work best for audiences in a single location versus those that are more effective for remote or mobile employees. We also discussed how you can use more than one vehicle to deliver a set of messages, such as an e-mail memo with an attached presentation.

The five most common myths about internal communications included a common misperception that only large companies communicate with employees. Small companies must also communicate with their employees. While that internal environment might not be as complex as in a larger company, it includes many of the same challenges that large companies face.

Quiz Yourself

1. There are two main types of corporate communications: external and internal.

- True. External communications are directed to customers and prospective customers, members of the media, prospective employees, and partners. Internal communications are directed towards employees and in some cases also to partners.

- False. Corporate communications consists of many types of communications, such as annual reports, Web pages, and e-mails.

2. Corporate storytelling is basically just internal public relations, lots of fluff and hype to try to get employees to do things management wants.

- True. Corporate storytelling is the practice of using fiction in employee communications.
- False. Corporate storytelling refers to the practice of using proven storytelling techniques — such as observation, careful selection of details, and audience awareness — to improve employee communications.

3. You should have a background in English or journalism if you want to implement the techniques in this book.

- True. Employee communications is a complex topic and the principles we're covering in this book are complex.
- False. Employee communications is not rocket science; it's based on common sense and a few, simple principles.

4. Internal communications isn't just for big companies; little companies grapple with the same problems, just on a slightly different scale.

- True. All sizes of companies must communicate with employees in a timely and accurate fashion about many things.
- False. Only big companies communicate with employees.

ANSWERS: 1. True 2. False 3. False 4. True

The Basics: Who

At the most basic level, your planning and development activities start and end with your audience, the target of your communication. By understanding your audience and your communications objectives for that audience, you will be able to make the most appropriate decisions concerning messages, media, frequency, and deliverables. You will be able to design a plan with clear objectives and then develop tactics to help you meet them.

Without a good understanding of your target audience — or access to somebody with that understanding — there's no way you can create a communication that will convey information in a meaningful way for those people. You will be sending messages in the dark and hoping a few of them reach their marks. So start with the people you are trying to reach.

You might not know anything about your target audience. Or, you might think you know everything. In this chapter, we'll look at steps you can take either to validate what you think you know or gain information that you're missing. We'll also discuss how this information about your target audience will influence numerous aspects of your plan.

Who Are You Trying to Reach?

What do they care about? How do they get their information now? What are their information needs? Start by naming your audience — perhaps you have more than one — and by describing their characteristics.

There are a million ways to capture this information. In my experience a summary matrix format is the most useful (see Figure 1). Matrices are easy to scan and let you spot patterns and also gaps — places where you don't have information but need it.

Matrices are typically created in spreadsheets, so they are easy to modify and sort to analyze different

Audience Assessment Summary Matrix

Figure 1

	Audience 1	Audience 2	Audience 3
Description			
Characteristics:			
Language			
Cultural factors			
Line of business factors			
Historical factors			
Information needs			
Media preferences			
Messenger preferences			
Alternate channels			
Key objective of comunication			
Tactics for key objective			
Known challenges			
Key milestones and messaging needs			
Other objectives/tactics			

patterns across audience segments. Each communications project has its own set of priorities and issues, again typically related to the target audiences but also due to the very nature of the project and the type of content that will need to be communicated.

Using matrices lets you set up a format that is consistent, but can be easily modified from project to project to meet varying needs. The objective is to quickly and effectively capture the information you need to create and execute a communications program that will be valuable to the people it is intended to address.

Some analysis systems ask you to create your audience analysis using a narrative descriptive format similar to a white paper (see Figure 2).

Audience Assessment — Narrative Format　　　Figure 2

Executive Summary
(This should summarize the entire analysis so that if someone were to read only this section of the paper, he or she would know what your recommendations are and why.)
Description of Target Audience(s)
(Details such as size, location, language(s), lines of business, and role(s) of audience(s).)
Communication Objective(s)
(State the communications objectives for the audience(s).)
What Is the Context?
(Information about how the message topic(s) fits into the company's history and current business direction.)
Overview of Current Messaging Patterns
(Details such as existing communications structures and patterns of messaging such as media preferences, messaging levels, messenger preferences, etc. Include specific executives, managers, and supervisors who are recognized messengers. Include specific company media such as the sales Web site or 4th floor bulletin board.)
Challenges
(Describe the factors specific to audience that will inhibit communication efforts.)
Risks
(Describe the risks of not meeting, or of trying but failing, to meet those challenges.)
Plan of Action
(Outline recommended plan, including tactics, for each objective. Address potential challenges and include a short-term set of action steps that can move planning work forward. This section can include cost, resource, and overall timing estimates.)

The benefit of this approach is that you can easily go into considerable detail about your audience's preferences, prior experiences, and possible hurdles to reaching them effectively. The challenge, though, is to extract the data from such a report into a usable plan of action.

You can, of course, use a blended approach in which you conduct your analysis and record your observations, details, and considerations in the narrative form and then extract the most important items and use them in summary form in the matrix for planning and development purposes.

If you have limited time to conduct any analysis, I recommend that you use the matrix approach and keep an idea list to capture comments and observations that seem interesting or troublesome but not quite ready to be dealt with (see Figure 3).

Idea List	Notes	Type
1	(Note possible uses, impacts, questions related to idea.)	(Indicate who, what, when, where, why)
2		
3		
4		
5		
6		
7		
8		
9		
10		
11		
12		
13		
14		
15		

Figure 3

Three Simple Tips for Conducting an Audience Analysis

1. Become familiar with the proposed topic of the communications.

While the audience is the foundation on which to plan and execute any internal communications activities, an audience analysis must take place within some sort of context. What is it that is going to be communicated to these people? Will it be about benefits policies or about a new application that will soon be in use? Perhaps the subject matter has to do with sales tools, such as product literature or availability data. You need to understand the proposed topic of your communications to some extent — not necessarily in exhaustive detail at this point, but to some extent.

In some organizations or projects, this means obtaining a copy of a scope document or reviewing material posted on a Web site or other information repository. It might mean making arrangements to join project team meetings on a regular basis. In a smaller company, it might mean setting up a half-hour meeting with the sponsoring executive or a member of their team.

2. Whatever your topic is, ask specific questions to obtain more accurate answers.

If your topic deals with benefits-related content, for example, you want to focus your analysis so that you gain an understanding of how your audience gets benefits-related information today, at what frequency, and to what end. Benefits information might very well be delivered differently than content about an application or sales incentive program. You want to attune your communications program to the audience's current expectations about receiving benefits information. The more specifically and precisely you can understand the environment your audience works and moves in, the more precisely and accurately you will be able to craft and distribute your communications to them.

3. Evaluate how well you know the target audience.

In a small company, you might know the target recipients very well and not need too much additional information as to their current preferences or existing media options. If you are new to the company or if the company is relatively large, you might not know the audience(s) well at all. In either case, it is a good idea to at least test your assumptions with people who are engaged on a daily basis with the targets. These people are called subject matter experts or audience experts. If you aren't at all familiar with the target audiences, you will want to conduct more extensive interviews with your audience experts.

Eight Steps to Validate Your Audience Analysis or Gain the Information You Need

To validate your assumptions about the audience and recommended course of action, take the following steps:

1. Complete an initial audience analysis, either in matrix or narrative format.

2. Note the areas of the analysis where you think expert input will be most valuable.

3. Identify people who are experts on the characteristics of your audience(s) and who can be expected to be able to answer some of your key questions in the analysis.

4. If it is at all possible, consider including actual audience members in your analysis.

5. Outline the top 5 to 10 questions or topics you would like to discuss with each expert. These questions should track directly to sections of your audience analysis and either validate your assumptions or provide input in areas where you need help (see Figure 4).

6. Prepare a 2 to 5 minute overview of why you are conducting this analysis and what roles the experts are playing in helping you complete the analysis. Consider each expert and how much, or how little, understanding they might have in the topics you will be addressing in your communications activities. Some experts might require more background information than others.

7. Arrange to speak with each expert for no more than half an hour. It is best to conduct this sort of interview one-on-one as opposed to holding a group session, for two reasons:

- In a one-on-one conversation, it will be easier to follow up on comments.

- In group settings, there are typically people who always speak and others who never speak; it is important that you get equitable input from all audience representatives or experts.

8. Be sure to send an e-mail to each audience expert, thanking them for their time and input. It's also wise to politely reserve the right to contact them again in the future to clarify or add to their comments.

If you aren't able to talk directly with your experts, you can ask them to validate your analysis using e-mail or a hard copy of the form. This method can be less than satisfactory, for two reasons. You won't be able to ask immediate follow-up questions. And written answers are often less complete than conversational answers; people rarely take the time to fully answer a question in writing while conversation moves more quickly and can cover more ground.

Audience Assessment: Interview Form

Intro	Brief overview of what you're doing and how the interviewee can help.
	Opportunity for interviewee to ask questions.
Q1	Your first question.
	Interviewee response and notes on follow-up discussion.
Q2	Your second question.
	Repeat as above for each question.
Q3	Your third question.
Q4	Your fourth question.
Q5	Your fifth question.
Q6	Your sixth question.
Q7	Your seventh question.
Q8	Your eighth question.
Q9	Your ninth question.
Close	Wrap conversation: Thank you for your input. That's all the questions I have for you today. I would appreciate it if I could contact you again if other questions arise. Is there anything else you'd like to add that we haven't covered?
	Interviewee response and notes on final follow-up discussion.

Figure 4

If you require more than just validation of your audience analysis, take the following steps:

1. Identify your probable audience(s).

2. Identify people who are experts on the characteristics of your audience(s) and who can be expected to be able to answer some of your key questions in the analysis.

3. If it is possible to interview actual members of your target groups, that would be ideal. Often, you must coordinate that with managers and supervisors to ensure that the team's workload is not adversely affected by interrupting a member's schedule.

4. Continue with steps 5 through 8, above.

The main difference between these two checklists is that in the first scenario, you are an audience expert and so you can complete an initial version of the analysis and then review that analysis with other experts. In the second scenario, you aren't an audience expert and so you generally identify your target audience(s) and then outline an interview approach that will elicit enough detailed input from the audience experts so that you can complete the audience analysis.

In either case, the interview is an application of journalism techniques used in investigative reporting, celebrity interviews, regular interviews, columns, features, and so on. The concept is simple: the reporter gains access to someone who is an expert in the topic at hand. The reporter then uses that time with the expert well to produce sound pieces of information that can be used to tell a fact-based story in a newspaper or magazine or on TV.

For the purposes of internal business communications, the reporter is the analyst — you. And your purpose is to gain solid, fact-based information to allow you to create credible and effective communications to inform and advise your target audience. Like the reporter, however, you must be able to apply basic interviewing techniques.

Five Basic Interview Techniques You Can Put to Use Immediately

1. Be prepared!

You need to know enough about your expert and his or her area of expertise relative to your project to be able to ask effective questions. For example, you would not want to ask technical, or IT, questions of a personnel expert.

At the same time, however, you don't need to know all that much in order to conduct highly successful interviews. Some of my most memorable and most successful business interviews have been with people about whom I knew very little. I also knew very little about the business environment in which they worked. But I did know a little something about some of the frustrations they had been experiencing and which the project I was involved with was supposed to help solve. In cases such as this, it is usually very useful to be candid with your experts. Tell them you don't have a strong background in a certain area and that you look forward to their help in getting a better understanding of it.

2. Ask leading, open-ended questions.

You want your expert to talk to you. Straight yes-or-no questions won't elicit a conversation, and it is from conversations that you will learn the most.

3. Listen, listen, listen!

It can be very tempting for an interviewer to get into a two-way conversation with their interview subject, but that is a mistake. Your goal as an interviewer is to encourage the interview subject to feel comfortable speaking with you and, in turn, give you lots of information. You will accomplish this not by sharing your information but by offering your subject an interested, attentive, and engaged audience. If you find yourself saying more than three sentences in row, other than at the very beginning and ending of the interview, you are talking too much. And that means you aren't listening.

4. Always be sensitive to the fact that there are many other demands on your interview subjects' time.

They have agreed to talk with you as a professional courtesy, and doing so takes time out of their already busy day. Also, if you notice that your interviewee appears distracted or unfocused, it's a good idea to ask if there might be a better time to meet or speak. Schedules and priorities change all the time, and there might very well be a critical business or even personal situation that must be dealt with first, in order for the subject to be able to focus on your questions and topic.

5. Leave your ego at home.

Interview subjects come in all flavors, including brusque, insulting, overbooked, and arrogant, to name just a few. It's important as an interviewer and audience analyst that you not take any of that personally. If you find yourself interviewing an apparently uncooperative subject, be nonplussed. Often, brusque and grumpy interview subjects, once they find they can't scare you off, actually turn out to be your best sources of information. If in fact the interview ends up being nonproductive, don't worry. You might uncover all you need from other interviews. In the worst case, you might need to find a different person to speak with you about a particular audience aspect.

Pencil Versus Tape Recorder

On a purely practical note about interviews, it can be very challenging to listen as carefully as you need to and simultaneously take good notes. For that reason, many people record their interviews. Others invite a second person to join them in the interview to help take notes. Yet others are excellent multitaskers and take their own notes.

Whichever method you prefer, it's a good idea to let the interview subject know that you will be taking notes and how you plan to use them. If someone else has joined you and will be taking notes, be sure to introduce them to the interview subject. It can be unsettling to answer questions while some unknown person scribbles away. And if you decide to record the conversation, remember that you must advise the other party that you are recording the conversation. You should also remember to allow time in your schedule to transcribe the recording into your notes.

A Quick Comment about Focus Groups

Focus groups are controlled settings that are similar in many ways to group interviews. There is typically a facilitator, participants, and observers. Often the focus group is videotaped and audiotaped. And the purpose of the focus group, just as with an interview, is to solicit information from the participants, who are deemed to be expert in their understanding of some issue related to the project, new product introduction, or corporate policy change. Despite these similarities, the type of input that you need at this point in your communications planning efforts is not the type of information you will obtain in group interview settings, including focus groups.

Focus groups also require considerable effort and cost. And while you will hear interesting dialog among participants regarding the planned communications efforts (and even more probably about the planned project or policy change), you probably won't get the specifics you need, which means you will have to conduct follow-up interviews. Also, you will probably exit the focus group with lots of information about certain audience segments or aspects and virtually none about others. Group settings are easily dominated by one or two personalities while others manage to remain virtually invisible. In a one-on-one situation, you can address that problem head-on.

What Will I Have By the End of This Audience Analysis?

Once you have conducted all the interviews, you will want to compile the raw data into a single document for tracking purposes and then summarize your findings in a narrative format similar to Figure 2 or in a matrix format along the lines of Figure 1.

But more importantly, by the end of the audience analysis you should be able to answer these questions:

- What are the key characteristics of your principal audience? And how can these characteristics be expected to impact communications?

- Is there more than one audience, and if so what are the critical differences and the resulting recommended segmentations?

- How should message content be tailored differently from segment to segment? Will timing also be affected?

- What media types and messaging frequency are most suitable for each audience segment?

- When should communications start and end for each segment?

- What are the key message strategies, i.e., what does each segment really care about and need to know? And what key differences exist from segment to segment?

- Who should deliver what types of messages to these audiences? Are there different deliverers for each segment?

- What hurdles exist to communicating on this topic to these groups?

- What are some ways that these hurdles can be overcome?

- What are some of the key assumptions, dependencies, and risks associated with communicating on this topic to these people?

- What distribution challenges potentially exist?

It's important to remember that though you might be able to summarize all kinds of things very nicely, you won't necessarily have all the answers you need yet to make the communications program happen. That's not the purpose of the audience analysis.

The analysis is to help you understand the target audience(s) and the communications environment in which they exist. With this understanding, you can build a plan that takes strengths and weaknesses of that environment into account, and eventually craft specific messages and communications deliverables that are most suited to their intended recipients.

Conduct an Audience Analysis, Leap a Hurdle or Two!

In the course of the analysis, you will probably come across factors that can't work well together or that will impact the degree to which you can reach a given audience. That's the point! Use this information to try to change those factors to be more hospitable.

For example, you might have discovered that the

audience segmentation for a communications project about a new benefits policy would be best if it could very detailed and specific.

• One of your audience experts has explained that there are subtle but important differences in how the new plan will affect telemarketing employees versus online customer support employees.

• However, based on input from another expert, you suspect that it will be virtually impossible to generate e-mail distribution lists consisting either of only telemarketers or only online customer support reps. These employees all belong to the same business unit and no distinctions have ever been needed for business reasons, so the capability to physically separate them using e-mail does not exist.

The distribution problem, then, is a potential hurdle to communicating to these two audiences in the desirable degree of detail. Because your analysis identified this potential hurdle, you can then advise the project's leaders that it exists and they can make an informed decision to address it.

• Perhaps the company's business leaders will agree that creating the capability to target these two subgroups individually is important and worth the investment that will be required.

• On the other hand, the business leaders might just as easily accept that communications won't be as targeted as originally desired and expectations will have to be altered accordingly.

In the second instance, you will probably want to explore secondary messaging options that will allow more detailed information to be available to those who want it, whether as part of an education package, as a download from a generally accessible Web site, or a printed handout from the unit's HR representative.

Obviously, either decision will affect your communications efforts:

- In the first instance above, you will be able to distribute the details to each audience in one coordinated move.

- In the second, you will either leave unfilled information gaps or have more to orchestrate. To try to fill the gaps that can't be detailed in the general e-mail that will be received by both audience segments, you could use the company's existing HR network to distribute more detailed communications to those who request them. Thus, the number of communications deliverables and steps recipients would have to take to access those materials increases:

  ✠ There would be an e-mail announcement. In addition to giving recipients an overview of the impending changes, it would also list contact information for HR representatives who could provide more detailed information.

  ✠ Those contacts would receive other materials, also probably created by you and targeted to the distinct audiences and available on request.

This situation is actually very common. It is also not particularly desirable because it requires that a more general, less relevant message be sent to a broad collection of recipients. Those recipients then must take a second or even third action to obtain the truly relevant information they actually need and can use. As a result, it is riskier in that fewer recipients can be expected to complete those extra actions without being reminded, which means that the communications effort might fail to accomplish its business goal.

To try to offset this risk, communications managers will often supplement their plan with a reminder communication to help drive completion of the desired actions on the part of the recipients. But again, since there's no way to target this reminder; everybody will receive it, including those people who have already taken the steps needed to get the information they need.

In the end, while it was not a communications problem per se that has created this scenario, the perception will be that there were too many communications to recipients on this subject and still the desired outcome did not happen.

Taking the steps to complete a thorough audience communications analysis early in the overall process can help identify this sort of issue. The earlier it's identified, the more likely it can be resolved. And at the very least, all involved parties will understand ahead of time why the communications must happen in a less-than-optimal manner. Meanwhile, you will have the basic and essential ingredients to crafting as thoughtful and effective a plan and set of deliverables as possible.

An Audience Analysis
Is Never Truly Finished

Your initial audience analysis is just the starting point. As you proceed through the other steps outlined in this book, be prepared to return to your audience analysis and update it. You'll notice over time that the work you do here influences and improves your ability to answer other communications questions farther down the road.

And don't make the mistake of thinking that everything matters. It doesn't. Storytellers only include the details that matter to the story they are telling, and you must do the same. If you're not sure, especially at this early stage in the process, log the information on one of the forms you're using. But when you start to summarize and recommend, make decisions and choices. You'll have to live by those decisions and choices later when you actually begin communicating. The analysis work you're doing here lays the foundations and guidelines that will allow you to prioritize messages so that you convey those details that really matter for your audience — the readers of your corporate story.

Of course, before you can prioritize details, you have to identify them, which is what we'll focus on in the *What* section — coming up next!

Now, take a few minutes to review this chapter's key points on the next page. Then take a short quiz.

Key Points

The most important point of this chapter is your audience, the *Who* of your communications plan. We reviewed why it is so important that you understand their information needs and current messaging patterns and preferences. We looked at several formats that you can use to record an audience analysis, and we looked at the eight steps you need to take to complete that analysis. Whether you choose to record your analysis in a matrix format or a narrative format doesn't really matter. What matters is that you develop a way of collecting and summarizing information about your audience that allows you to reuse this information later to create actual messages and communications.

Part of the analysis process is to interview audience experts, who are more knowledgeable about your target audience. Use the five interview tips in this chapter to optimize your limited time with the experts. Whether you decide to record your interviews or just take notes, ensure that your interview subject is aware of and comfortable with your method.

Audience experts are extremely valuable, extended members of your team whom you will want to contact later with very focused questions to help you refine your plan or an actual memo or Web page.

While you might be tempted to conduct a group interview with your experts or a sort of focus group to save time, beware! Group interviews aren't the same as focus groups and neither will give you the opportunities for follow-up questioning that you want in an analysis discussion.

By the end of this process, you will have a good understanding of your audience in context of the particular project you're supporting. This is not an end-state, but the initial point of what should be an iterative, or ongoing, process. As you continue to gain information about your project or company and how it will affect the target audiences, you will need to return to this analysis and update it.

In addition to giving you vital information about your audience and how they need to receive information, the audience analysis can also pinpoint hurdles that you will have to overcome in your planning and execution steps. Sometimes you will be able to remove the hurdle without impacting the quality of the communication. Other times, the hurdle might be immovable, and you will have to modify your communication goals or plan to accommodate the limitations it imposes.

Quiz Yourself

1. The purpose of an audience analysis is to document everything you know about the people who will receive your communications.
- True. It's your point of view that matters.
- False. It's your chance to collect information from many sources and then synthesize it.

2. An audience analysis is just a formality. If you already know your employees pretty well, you really don't need to do it. Just go right on to making a list of key messages.
- True. Don't waste your time on all this busywork.
- False. The analysis allows you to supplement your own personal information and also validate key assumptions with other experts.

3. An audience analysis can be documented in a highly detailed format, like a white paper, or it can be documented in a matrixed format that is easy to scan and modify.

- True. Format does not really matter as long as the data is easy to access and understandable by you and your coworkers.
- False. The audience analysis must be documented in a very specific and technical way or else it won't be recognized.

4. The more detailed your audience analysis, the better your communications plan will be.

- True. It's better to collect every single detail no matter how small or questionable in value.
- False. Having the right details is what matters — and not all details actually matter.

5. Once you complete the audience analysis, that's it. You're ready to write the newsletter or memo or Web page.

- True. As long as you have thought a little bit about your audience's priorities and points of view, then you can get going.
- False. In addition to understanding your audience well, you must also understand the project, new policy or other communications topics well enough to convey salient details to the people affected.

ANSWERS: 1. False 2. False 3. True 4. False 5. False

The Basics: What

While you're analyzing your audience, you must also understand what you're going to be communicating to them.

Suppose it's an IT project. What is its name and when will it start? How long will it last, and what will be the outcome? What legacy systems will be updated or replaced? What will be the new system's advantages over the older one? Who will get the system first, and how long will deployment take?

If it's a newsletter or other effort designed to help drive sales, what type of sales are being sought? Is the focus on new business or is it on a certain industry? Perhaps there is a competition. What are the competition dates? How do you enter, and what criteria will determine the winners? How many winners will there be? What is the prize?

If your topic deals with new benefits or employee policies, what are they, exactly? What is the scope of the changes? Is everyone affected equally, or does it vary?

What are the variables? What actions will people have to take and in what time frame?

You must know the facts about your project. Some of those facts might already be determined, while others must wait until the project or initiative matures further. But you need to be asking the questions necessary to uncover, collect, and document those facts so you can communicate them when the time is right.

In this chapter, our focus is on how to identify different types of questions and then use them to gain specific types of information to help you plan and communicate.

Look For Large "Whats" and Small "Whats"

With almost any communication effort, you must understand your topic on at least two different levels: large and small, strategic and tactical. The large, or strategic, facts have to do with how your topic applies to or affects virtually all audience segments. These messages will be more general and broader than small, or tactical, facts. They will relate directly to the company or division's vision. And they will convey how the new IT system, or benefits package, or sales initiative will help the company achieve its market-oriented goals.

Tactical pieces of information deal directly with the world of the individual recipient. What steps are being taken to get this new IT system or benefits package to employees? What do employees need to do to take advantage of it or to comply with the new employee policies? To be ready to use the new IT system? To compete and win in the new sales environment?

Large "whats" convey the bigger picture, while small "whats" convey the granular, or nitty-gritty, details that compose that picture.

Strategic facts are very useful at the beginning of internal communication programs. They help set a context for the project or initiative. They establish a foundation of the audience's general, shared awareness and eventual understanding. It's vital that this context be established at the start and then reinforced throughout the communication cycle.

Very quickly, however, tactical information becomes critically important. However, these are often the most difficult messages to pin down precisely and succinctly. Sometimes, tactical messages become more defined as a project matures. Sometimes there are so many tactical facts that choosing among them seems impossible. Sometimes, however, there is simply a dearth of tactical facts because the project or program you are supporting has not been well defined. In any scenario, however, the job of the communicator — the storyteller — is the same: know your audience and focus on the facts that do exist!

The Facts, Please

Whether strategic or tactical, the facts about your project are the meat of your messages. If you are low on facts, your communications will be low on value and high on fluff. It's impossible to emphasize enough how important it is to let facts drive your communications. If you don't have the facts, don't try to communicate as if you do. Instead, focus on filling in the blanks: get the facts, get them straight, and send your audience information that provides some degree of value to them.

Frankly, getting the facts clearly and compellingly

articulated can be hard to do. While there is often a huge amount of information about a project or new policy, there is often a dearth of accessible, tangible, informative, accurate facts.

Why is that? Because projects and policies can be funded, resourced, and even implemented without answering many of the hard questions organizations and employees face every day. Scope documents can be written so that they specifically don't address thorny problems, for example. And recurring issues can often be sidelined during a project's lifespan by naming them dependencies in a project plan and making them someone else's problem.

But when it comes time to communicate about the new dress code or flextime policies or compensation changes, you have to address the hard questions and the overlooked or pushed-aside details — because those are the questions most thinking, reasonable employees will immediately raise. So you might as well ask them first!

Sometimes, by asking those questions, you drive old, unresolved issues out into the open where they can't be glossed over or hidden. The point is not to expose team members as incompetent or even to resolve every one of those irritating issues. The point is to identify what it is that needs to be communicated so that you can be specific in the communications you develop and employees will know what questions are being answered and which ones aren't.

Of course, many issues in a project or initiative will remain thorny, and you will have to communicate around them, in spite of them, and sometimes in defiance of them. But the more facts you can provide or issues you can directly address, the more credible your communication will be to recipients. If you avoid known hot topics and act as if they don't exist, your communications will seem incomplete and even inaccurate, and your messages won't reach their intended audience.

Watch Out for Those "Heads-up" Communications!

Project teams and leaders are often overeager to issue missives to the masses about their latest project or milestone made. That is not a good idea, in most circumstances.

Issuing a "fluffy" communication to meet a project team or sponsoring executive's agenda might make you or your project leader look good on paper, but rest assured it won't fool — or inform — anyone. The communication won't provide value; it probably won't be read; and it will lower audience expectations about what they can expect to learn from future communications from the same source. And that will make your task in the future just that much more difficult to accomplish.

Face the Facts . . . But First, Find Them

Collecting and choosing the right facts is probably one of the most difficult parts of communicating about anything — internally or externally, in business or in other professions.

Journalists grapple with facts every day; it's a major part of their job. Being able to ask good questions, listen well, find reliable sources, and put together pieces of the puzzle are characteristics of a good journalist. They're also vital for corporate storytellers. Writing is almost the last step in the process of creating an article or column — or a memo — and it has to be done well. But if there is no information to communicate — or it's not the right information — then there is nothing to write.

Advertising copywriters and public relations writers,

on the other hand, are adept at making something out of nothing. Unfortunately, many business communicators try this tactic too — without success. Because even ads and press releases are more effective when they're founded on something solid. Think of which newspaper ads you respond to: the ones for a store you like offering a product you want to purchase, maybe at a good discount.

These are all facts — pieces of information that the reader or viewer can receive and then choose to act on. Communications about ideas or intentions or descriptions of strategies aren't communicating facts. They aren't actionable. They probably won't engage a reader. They might work if delivered in person or even on a conference call or other large meeting venue where the energy of engagement can drive them forward. But even then, once the meeting or conference is over, recipients need to be able to go back to the workplace and do something with those messages. Act on them. Incorporate them into their daily work lives.

Even the most strategic, idea-oriented messages must come down to earth in the end. And since real information is the hardest content to find and finalize, start early in your communications work to gather the facts. Decisions about prioritizing that data, as well as positioning and packaging it will come later. But if you don't have the basics in hand, there will be nothing to position or package.

Three Tips for Collecting and Choosing the Perfect Facts!

A corporate storyteller, like a novelist or scriptwriter, is driven by three criteria: audience, action, and timeline.

1. Know who you are writing for and what they are interested in or will expect. That's why that audience analysis is so vital.

2. Understand what you will be communicating about: your topic and how it will affect each audience segment.

3. Understand what different information will be needed at different times.

Note that every one of these directives contains a *what*. Note also how *who* and *what* connect in the first, and in the third there is a link between *what* and *when*. This is an important illustration of how closely related the Five Ws are.

Devise a Low-maintenance Method to Record and Track These Facts, By Audience.

Let's say your project is an IT implementation that affects several audiences. You have determined that the audience segments will need general information at first. But, as time passes, they will need increasingly tactical information such as training and how to prepare their workstations. And you have discovered that these details and their timing are likely to vary considerably for each segment. You will have to keep these factors very clear in your planning and execution activities.

At this point in the project, you are simply collecting information. Eventually, you will select those facts that are most useful and informative for each audience segment.

You know that providing too much information will create clutter and confusion, while too little will leave people unable to complete crucial steps that will affect deployment. You must develop a method to track and sort the data that you collect, quickly and easily, as you expect it to change frequently.

Project Basics Note that some information will be sensitive, even for internal use.	Organization	Audience 1	Audience 2
Project or initiative sponsor.			
Executive sponsor(s).			
Overall start date and expected duration.			
Vendors involved and their role(s).			
Market or offerings implications.			
Project objectives.			
Expected corporate/divisional benefits or ROI.			
Expected time frame for corporate or divisional benefits or ROI.			
Total audience affected.			
Detailed audience info (include numbers).			
Which people in the named divisions are affected?			
Front-line employees			
Managers/supervisors			
Territory executives			
Administrative staff			
Operational staff (add other areas as needed)			
Are all regions affected? (Note timing variables for regions.)			
Do specific job or division codes apply? (specify for each segment)			
What will happen.			
In general terms when is the project expected for each audience segment? (Note expected duration.)			
Will people receive: New hardware?			
New software?			
New IDs?			
Education?			
Paperwork that must be completed?			
What actions will people have to take? (Time period?)			
What can audiences expect in terms of workflow disruption, if any?			
What impact is expected on customers?			
What impact is expected on partners?			
What will change.			
What applications in use today will be sunset? (Provide schedule and other details for each.)			
What forms or other aids in use today will be sunset? (Provide schedule and other details for each.)			
What business processes in use today will change? (Provide schedule and other details for each.)			

Figure 5

There are many ways to accomplish this. If you're very closely involved in the project about which you'll communicate, you might already know what the project is and how it will affect people. There might be a scope document you can extract information from. There might be phone calls you can join in and take notes about. There might be people you can interview and catch up with. You might have a notebook that you will keep all this information in. You might use a white board. But if you work with a remote team, it will be helpful to have a soft-copy version of your notes about what this project is. The table in Figure 5 contains common questions that you can adapt for your own project. The matrix format will allow you to note variations among the audiences.

Organize Data Into Message Families

Message families are sets of messages that all deal with a common theme or topic as shown in Figure 6.

Message Matrix Cross-reference which messages apply to which audiences and if modication is required.	Audience 1	Audience 2	Audience 3
Message family #1			
Message #1			
Message #2			
Message #3			
Message #4			
Message family #2			
Message #1			
Message #2			
Message #3			
Message #4			
Message family #3			
Message #1			
Message #2			
Message #3			
Message #4			

Figure 6

For example, a message family for an IT rollout might be education or deployment. For a sales incentive program, it might be the program's time period or the prizes offered.

Organizing message fragments into families will help you identify ways to consolidate messages and will also help you separate the wheat from the chaff. As we've discussed in earlier chapters, not all details are important to the story that you're trying to tell. Collecting data in message families allows you to track information pieces and prioritize them without entirely losing them.

As with the audience analysis, you'll find that you return again and again to your collection of "whats." The iterative nature of communicating is important and valuable. With each return, you'll find that you've understood more than before and that you've gained practical insight that will help you communicate more specifically and accurately.

What Is Your Communication Objective?

The other aspect of thinking strategically about the "what" of your topic is to identify what role the communications will play. You must be able to answer these and similar questions:

- What are your communications objectives for this project, and what tactics will you employ to accomplish each goal?

- What business problem is being addressed by the introduction of a new benefits package or IT system?

- How will communications help resolve that problem?

- What criteria will be used to determine whether you've been successful?

Good Objectives Are Measurable!

That said, remember that it can be very hard to measure the impact of communications in most business environments. The following common measurement methods are options you will want to consider.

Surveys

Drawbacks to using surveys are several. For one thing, they take people's time away from their jobs, which bosses don't usually like. Survey language and analysis is a very specialized type of work that is costly to implement.

Internal surveys are often constructed by people with good intentions, who know lots about their company but little about statistics or survey analysis, The results of such surveys are questionable at best since survey questions are often poorly worded and not quantifiable. In these cases, survey populations are also often not truly representative of the target audience or of the right size to project a statistically meaningful conclusion.

Audit of Messages Sent and Messages Received

E-mail programs can often monitor and track message distribution, confirm receipt, and also confirm that the recipient opened the e-mail. Web sites can be designed to monitor visits, visitors, time spent, pages visited, time of visit, and other user statistics. Companies often have restrictions and costs associated with these devices, as they require programming expertise and will impact a Web site or server structure.

Compliance With a Requested Action

For example, if a communication asked recipients to enroll in a certain education course, you can monitor the number of enrollments within a certain period of the communication's distribution.

Similarly, perhaps recipients were asked to visit a specific Web page and download and new set of instructions for their immediate use. You can monitor traffic to that Web page to evaluate the level of compliance that results from the communication.

Timeliness, Accuracy, Frequency

The preceding measurements focused on measuring the affect of communications based on actions taken or not taken by the target population. Another type of objective relates to the parameters of the communications themselves. Here are several examples.

- Communications will deliver business value, which is defined as: delivering accurate, fact-based messages that provide actionable information relevant to the recipient. Measurements for this type of objective would include:

    ✠ The number of facts communicated and the number of percentage that were proven accurate to a certain scale, such as: 100 percent, 75 percent, less than 75 percent.

    ✠ Confirmation that an action was included in every single communication issued.

- Communications will be released to targets at least 48 hours before any action is required. The measurement would be:
  ✠ Confirmation that the communication was released to the audience at least two full days in advance of the action's required completion date.

- There will be no more than 5 communications on this topic to a given target within a 5-week period.
  ✠ Confirmation that this cap was not exceeded.

If You Can't Measure It, It's Not a Communications Objective That You Want to Be Responsible For

The most important things about communications objectives are that you have at least one, that is measurable and real, and that you have identified the tactics you will use to accomplish it. An objective such as "supporting the deployment of a new sales automation system to the front line" is not a real or measurable objective. Challenge yourself, within your organization's capabilities, to come up with an objective, or several objectives, that are specific, measurable, and valuable.

One of the most common, unmeasurable communications objectives is often found under the heading "Awareness." Beware!

Measuring whether a communications program has increased awareness or acceptance of a new policy is very difficult to accomplish without investment in feedback mechanisms such as audience surveys. You can monitor feedback or inquiries to agents within a company, such as a help desk, HR department, or collection of managers within the target audiences, but those sources will only be indicators, not truly statistically reliable measurements. And if you are being evaluated on how well such an "Awareness" communications program performs, you are likely to find yourself in an undefendable position.

Here's an example: You've been asked to increase awareness about a new sales incentive program in the northeast region. The current level of awareness has been described as "poor" based on conversations among the region's vice president and five territory managers, but here are the facts:

- No quantifiable surveys or other evaluations have been carried out.

- Sales performance has dropped 8 to10 percent in each of the preceding three years.

- Salespeople have been on record for at least 5 years with the complaint that the company's price point for its services is no longer competitive.

- The company initiated a sales incentive program last year that was not well received and didn't produce the desired results.

- The incentive program is a corporate program, and the regions must use it.

- This year's incentive program is a major agenda item for the division's general manager, to whom the regional vice president reports.

- The program itself is not a lot different than the

one introduced last year, though it has a new name, new logo, and new director.

• Corporate does not provide much funding or other assistance to communicate to sales reps about the program. All messages are delivered on a corporate Web site and are very broad in terms of the benefits promised.

• Your region's sales reps rarely spend time in their offices; they are usually on the road and don't have time to visit Web sites. They can barely keep up with e-mail from customers.

• You aren't allowed to contact sales reps directly but rather always work through their territory managers.

• Your assignment is to increase awareness among the sales reps.

This is a common scenario and what it really comes down to is whether you can change the territory managers' level of understanding so that they can convey the right information to their staff. The real problem here is to improve communication among management levels and then between line management and their employees. It's as much a leadership issue as it is a communication issue. And because you understand that distinction, you can create real and valuable objectives for communications rather than accept vast objectives that aren't measurable and that are beyond the scope of a communications program to address!

Using *What* questions to understand the project or initiative at hand will allow you to focus your efforts and also to identify truly useful information to convey to your targets. Very soon after you begin learning about your project and how it affects the audience, you will need to include *When, Where,* and *Why* questions, as well. And, we will discuss those next. However, it's critical that you spend a little extra time on *What*. Like *Who*, it is a very powerful communications planning and development tool.

Before you go on to the next chapter on *When, Where,* and *Why,* take a few minutes to review the key points we covered in this chapter and quiz yourself.

Key Points

We discussed what I call large "whats" and small "whats." These are the strategic and tactical aspects that you must understand about the project you're supporting. These facts will help you decide what you need to communicate to whom, when — and this is the basis of a communications plan.

What questions, of all sizes, are the questions that will help you find meaty, useful information for your communications. The answers you receive will range in value but will include big-picture pieces of information as well as tactical details that are especially pertinent to individuals, who really just want to know, "What's in it for me?"

There are some trouble spots to be aware of, too. Watch out for general "heads-up" communication requests and of setting general communication objectives that can't be measured. Both these things are examples of how easy it is to misuse employee communications. Heads-up communication that merely advertises the work of a certain team without providing any clear benefit to recipients of that communication are taking up unnecessary space in your schedule and for your audience. And if you are asked to make something like "increased awareness" one of your objectives, do everything you can to reword it so that you have a quantifiable, measurable objective. Awareness can be a catchall for all kinds of things that have nothing to do with communications.

We looked at three tips to help you collect and keep track of good, hard facts so that you can use them for each audience segment appropriately.

And we identified communications objectives that are measurable and valuable.

Quiz Yourself

1. Facts aren't that important until later in a project.
- True. At the beginning you want to generate good feelings about the project and too much information will just distract people.
- False. Facts are the meat of communications at all times in a project, whether they are more general facts or tightly detailed.

2. Too much information can be as useless as too little.
- True. Employees want to know what they need to know, when they need it.
- False. Getting more information than is needed is a good thing; people can always reference it later.

3. Large "whats" are the fluff.

● True. Large "whats" make up the filler that you tell people until you have all the details worked out.

● False. Large "whats" are the more strategic facts about a project or initiative; they apply to all audiences involved and are more general in nature.

4. Communication objectives must be measurable.

● True. Objectives that aren't measurable aren't of any value.

● False. Objectives can be of any type and don't have to be measurable to still provide value and help establish priorities.

The Basics:
When, Where, and Why

In this chapter, we're going to talk about three types of basic questions rather than take them one at a time. *When, Where,* and *Why* questions are usually so closely related that it makes sense to deal with them together. Let's look at how you can use them to uncover the details of your project as well as other elements that will affect your planning decisions.

Get the Nitty-gritty Details

In many ways, *When, Where,* and *Why* questions are extensions of *What* questions. Here are a few that allow you to quickly get to your project's details:

- When will the new benefits package be available?

- Where will people go to learn more or to enroll?

- Why is this new policy being offered now?

These questions will help you flesh out the message matrices we started to construct in the preceding chapter.

Get Help When You Need It

When, Where, and *Why* questions are great help in the planning process. They uncover

- Timing elements that will help define the literal structure of your plan: what messages need to be delivered to your audiences when?

- Media options that will affect where you choose to publish your messages.

- Motivational elements that will affect how you package and position messages

Timing Is Everything

The types of messages that need to be delivered earlier in a project are different from those that will be delivered later on.

For example, early on in an IT rollout you might want to make people aware that they will be receiving new software or hardware that will help them perform their jobs more easily. As the deployment period approaches, they will be asked to set aside time for cleaning up data records and performing other system updates. As the deployment draws still closer, they will need to undergo training. And, finally, if the system change requires any downtime or manual updates, they will need that information as well as information about where to get help with any problems.

Some of the questions you would ask in a project like this one would be:

- When will education be offered?

- Where will that education take place?

- Why will the training last two full days?

- When does the audience need to know about planned system outages?

- Where should people turn to get support during the implementation?

Understanding message timing goes directly back to our communication objective to provide business value to recipients and not information overload.

Fellow employees are busy enough with their daily work; very few need or want to know anything about projects or efforts that don't yet directly impact them. So, as a matter of respect and good communications practices, your job is to inform them when and to the degree that they need to be informed. Understanding how the project itself will unfold over time will help you accomplish that goal. Use *When, Where,* and *Why* questions to help you understand your project better.

Whoa! Easy does it, now

Consider carefully how much preparation your audience really needs, whether they're receiving a new benefits package, an IT system, or a business process. Each project is different, but when people speak of "preparing" audiences, often they are talking about generating "awareness," which we discussed in the preceding chapter.

What is the value to the audience of this heightened awareness? If you can't answer that, then it's a pretty safe bet that your audience won't get any value. General answers, such as "they'll understand what's going on better" aren't very valuable. Does the audience need to understand what's going on right now in the project any better? What are the specific information points that they need to receive information on, and what business value will that data provide?

Too much "preparation" can seriously backfire later in a project. If a project team has touted a new program for several months before its actual launch, users might be expecting something quite phenomenal and their expectations aren't likely to be met. This can make adoption of the new program slower than it would have been otherwise, and it can also negatively affect morale and work attitudes within the target audience.

Two Reminders to Help You Avoid Setting Unrealistic Expectations

Avoid talking too much about what will happen in the future.

When you talk about the future, you have probably moved away from the world of facts to the world of supposition. You have also moved away from communicating actionable information to communicating intentions and ideas. There's also the risk that you will reopen old, organizational wounds by pledging to address what employees recognize as long-standing, as-yet-unaddressed problems.

Avoid talking about any project or change very far in advance.

How can you know when you are communicating too far in advance? Apply the same criteria we have been using all along:

- Does the recipient *need* to know this information now in order to do their job or to continue to do their job?

- If the recipient doesn't receive this information now, will he or she be unable to continue or complete required activities now or in the near future?

There are at least two reasonable-sounding reasons why people want to tease audiences about their projects too far in advance:

- They want to get people's attention, which can be very difficult to do in the busy world we live in. They mistakenly believe that if they start to try to get people's attention earlier, that will help them get their messages across.

- They believe that it's necessary to start communicating very early, when hard data is often in short supply, to be sure that their audience understands all the reasons behind an impending change so that they can transition smoothly through the implementation activities.

These reasons aren't good enough! First, you won't get the attention that you want by sending memos or newsletters on topics that won't affect the recipients for months or even years. Second, you don't have to start helping people understand their role in a transition more than a few months before the event.

So be cautious when asked to prepare your audiences very far in advance, and stick to your framework of fact-based, accurate messages that inform and compel recipients to take the recommended action.

And take advantage of the organizational structures already in place, as opposed to issuing direct communications to every employee. If executives and eventually managers or supervisors are up-to-date with the organization's plans, they will ensure that front-line employees are informed in timely and appropriate fashion. It's a mistake to bypass that structure and directly communicate with front-line employees about something that is far off on the horizon.

Communicate Early, Say the Experts – But Not Too Early!

Many studies on internal communications advise readers to communicate often and early. But consider for a moment what that really means.

Say you have a project that will take three to four years to fully deploy across a global company. On that scale, then, often and early could be taken to mean that you should communicate to front-line employees about a pending project for two to three years before anything actually directly impacts them. How could that possibly be effective or efficient? In another example, you might be launching a new incentive program to 16 sales reps in your single-state company, in which early might mean the Tuesday before you implement the program.

By the same token, though, in the global example, certain members of the executive, operations, and management teams do need to know what is going over that complete three- to four-year period. Similarly, the managers of those 16 sales reps will need to know about and understand the new incentive program before it's announced and implemented.

The opposite extreme is just as foolish. You can't expect to deploy a new IT system without employees being prepared with new workstations and adequate training. They must be informed in time to acquire both. The challenge, as always, is balance. What needs to be communicated to whom, when, and by whom?

It is also a fact that people must come into contact with messages more than once to really retain them. Some sources say understanding or retention takes at least seven "touches." But the challenge isn't to begin communicating too far in advance; rather, you must simply create opportunities for that number of touches within a shorter, reasonable time span before the project begins to affect employees.

When you start communicating, create a drumbeat!

A drumbeat is a way of saying that communications are issued to employees on a regular frequency. A drumbeat sets up a level of expectation and understanding within target audiences that helps individuals absorb and retain the content of the messages you send.

It can be a very slow frequency, for example, or it can be more aggressive. A long-term project might decide to issue a monthly newsletter, for example, while a shorter project might issue five communications over a five-week period. You might decide to use different messaging frequencies during different stages of your project and your communications program.

Use Integrated Messaging Internally

So the drumbeat refers to how frequently new messages are issued. But what if you want to increase either the number of times that employees receive this message or the likelihood that employees receive the message at least once? You integrate your messages using multiple media or delivery vehicles.

In fact, there is no other way to increase frequency within a given time period. You must use multiple media and delivery methods.

And if your fellow employees appear to be inundated with e-mail and you aren't confident that they will read the e-mail that you send on this topic, then you must create more opportunities for them to see this content. You must use internal news services, the management and team structures, Web pages, and perhaps even handouts that can be dropped on desks.

By pushing messages using a number of different channels over a consecutive series of weeks or months, you will create a sort of drumbeat and recognizable set of messages about your project.

"Push" Versus "Pull" Communications

Communications aficionados will knowingly talk about balancing your plan with "push" and "pull" communications. What does that mean?

It's simple. "Push" communications are those that literally get pushed to employees, either through e-mail, handouts, telephone message, or management. "Pull" communications are those that employees have to go seek, such as Web pages.

If you use the integrated messaging approach that's described here you will have a useful balance of "push" versus "pull" messaging.

Using *Why* Questions to Find Motivational Factors

Why questions can unlock hidden communications opportunities for you. But beware! They aren't usually the source of good messages. The one exception is when a *Why* question illuminates a procedure that should or should not be done.

Most *Why* questions will uncover information that will help you position or package your communications. This information is known as benefits and will apply to a number of different levels within the organization. For example, you might be able to identify benefits for the company as a whole, for the specific division or operating unit, for the sales or manufacturing team, for the individual employee, for the partner, and for the customer.

Benefits usually take the shape of what the company values most: customer satisfaction, product or services ingenuity, increased revenue or market share, decreased costs, increased employee satisfaction and opportunity for growth, etc.

At the highest level, a common *Why* question would be: Why is the company introducing this sales incentive plan now? The answer could include a benefit to the company, such as: "Because we are 27 percent away from our year-end sales goal and we have to do everything we can to get there." And it could include a benefit to the individual: "This is the last quarter; we want to encourage our salespeople to go for broke and set new levels of excellence for themselves — and we'll reward them for succeeding."

Both of these benefits will have to be positioned and packaged to be useful in a communication. Perhaps the individual benefit will become part of a "quest for excellence" set of messages that are ongoing to the salespeople. And the corporate benefit will take the form of a challenge to turn the company's competitive edge toward the marketplace and toward winning.

In another scenario, suppose the company is replacing an inadequate IT system with a new one. In this case, we could ask virtually the same *Why* question: Why is the company investing in this IT system now? But the answer would be very different: Because the business needs information or capabilities that the current system can't deliver, and the company believes this new system will be able to accomplish both.

But from an individual's, and probably also a manager's, point of view, a new system means downtime for training, so articulating what the benefits are for managers and individuals will be very important — and probably difficult. You will have to find explicit examples of improved function or reporting, for example. And you can also expect that there will be areas of the new application that compare less favorably to the legacy system, so you will have to consider whether individuals will consider the new system a net improvement, no change, or perhaps even a net loss.

Asking good *Why* questions will help you to identify pockets of sensitivity or skepticism in audience communities. You might not be able to resolve that sensitivity or skepticism, but with awareness you can avoid exacerbating it. Good *Why* questions will also help you to zero in on the most important benefits: those to individuals, who basically want to know, "What's in it for me?"

Well, that's it for the Five Ws! The next chapter offers easy writing and design tips. But before you leave this chapter, take a few minutes to look over the key points that we just covered and then quiz yourself!

Key Points

The short version of this chapter is that *When, Where,* and *Why* questions are extensions of *What* questions. Use them to learn more about your project and your audiences.

You can also use *When, Where,* and *Why* questions

to influence your communications plan in terms of timing, media selection, and packaging. *Why* questions are particularly useful in uncovering motivational — or resistance — factors. But be careful of using them as straight messages. They typically fall more into the idea realm as opposed to facts, except for those *Why* questions that have to do with specific benefits or with instructions to do or not do a specific procedure.

When, where, and *why* questions can sometimes lead to the requirement of "preparing" audiences for a new application or other change. Consider such requirements very carefully before adding them to your plan. Communicating too far in advance is not only worthless in that people won't remember what you need them to remember, but you probably won't have the tactical level of detail that you really need to communicate to them. Communicate within reasonable time spans. Use integrated messaging techniques to increase "touches," and establish a clear, consistent drumbeat in which to deliver those messages. It will also automatically help you include a mixture of "push" and "pull" communications.

Avoid setting unrealistic expectations — one of the best techniques to use to do that is to rely heavily on fact-based messaging.

The most important type of message to uncover is the answer to *What's in it for me?*

Quiz Yourself

1. *When*, *Where*, and *Why* questions are basically just the same as *What* questions; you don't need to bother much with them at all.

- True. Focusing on the *What* questions is what matters.
- False. *When*, *Where*, and *Why* questions are similar to *What* questions, but they will provide more details about the project itself and about what audience segments really need to know, when.

2. Message families are collections of messages on a related topic, such as rollout or education.

- True. Using message families helps you to group common themes for easier tracking, updating, and cross-matching to audience segments.
- False. Message families is an arbitrary grouping of details based on audience relevance.

3. WIIFM stands for *What's In It For Management.*

- True. Management is always the most important audience segment to consider in any communications program.
- False. WIIFM stands for *What's In It For Me?* This refers to the primary question that most employees have in mind when they read a communication or hear about a new initiative, program, plan, etc.

4. The best way to increase the number of times a message touches an audience segment is to start communicating about a project as early as possible, even if that is months or even years before the project will actually impact the audience.

- True. You can never communicate too much to fellow employees, in general.
- False. It is disrespectful and wasteful of fellow employees' time to burden them with information that doesn't actually apply to them at the time that it's communicated.

5. *Why* questions can uncover useful pieces of information, but not always good messages.

- True. *Why* questions commonly uncover benefits and rationale behind projects, which can be very helpful when it comes to packaging and positioning messages to different audiences.
- False. Answers to *Why* questions make great messages that focus on ideas and intentions that are driving a project.

ANSWERS: 1. False 2. True 3. False 4. False 5. True

The Basics:
Writing and Page Layout Tips

There are many great sources of writing and page-design instruction available in bookstores, classrooms, and online. Take advantage of them!

But if you don't have time to take a course or if you just want a pointer or two, this section contains a few of the most important things you need to remember when it comes to writing or using design elements in your communications. There's also a short list of good resources at the end of the section.

The goal of good writing is to choose words and sentences that do the work you need them to do: convey information accurately, quickly, and easily. The following principles can help.

Show, Don't Tell

This is just another way of saying let your readers decide what they think themselves, rather than telling them what to think.

In fiction, this principle is used to dramatize stories by conveying action rather describing it. For example:

Telling: Terri told Ursula how she had used the big blue comb to fix her daughter Shelley's hair that morning, instead of the white one with the broken teeth.

Showing: "Oh dear me, no! I didn't dare use that mammoth white comb on Shelley-dear this morning," said Terri, as she minced white onions near the sink. "I found that lovely blue one that Kevin brought over from London last. It's so smooth and doesn't pull even a little bit. And Shelley just laughs to see the blue flash in the mirror, you know!"

In this example, using dialogue tells us a lot more about the character than simply narrating the action. That's because conveying action and immediacy engages readers far more that simply reciting details.

In business writing it's no different. Rather than describing an expected benefit, for example, articulate what is new or changed. If there is a benefit, it will be clear to your readers. And if it's marginal, no amount of benefits statements will change that fact. Trying to present a marginal benefit as a real one just irritates readers and erodes credibility. For example,

Telling: The team implementing a new benefits package proposed the following benefit statement for use in the announcement memo to employees about the new plan: *The new benefits package lets you take better care of your family and manage your benefits in less time than before.*

Showing: The reality of the new package, in fact, had nothing to do with actual benefits changes but with a change in how the plan options are managed. It looked like this: *With the new benefits package, you can change pension plan investments and health insurance selections directly and privately, and receive confirmation within 24 hours. You no longer need to submit changes to a benefits counselor and then wait ten days for confirmation.*

By stating the changes in a way that allowed the advantages to stand on their own, the project team avoided overpromising or misrepresenting their true scope, which is that employees now have more control over their pension investments and health insurance options. Whether the new package in fact saves them time or improves their ability to care for their family is open to debate. Consider the following supporting and non-supporting facts:

Original benefit statement	Supporting facts	Non-supporting facts
Saves time	No longer needs to wait or follow-up on actions of benefits counselor	Must now execute the change himself
Take better care of family	Can now change to a more appropriate plan as family circumstances change	Plan options are unchanged

Figure 7

Shorter is Harder but Better; Longer Is Easier but Not User-friendly

The great philosopher and mathematician Blaise Pascal once wrote to a friend: *I have made this letter longer only because I did not have time to make it shorter* (Lettres Provinciales, 1656-57).

Many people mistakenly believe that it takes more effort, more thought, and more time to write a long memo or presentation, or that the longer the memo, the more information it contains. Neither is true — unless the longer version actually contains more useful information than the shorter one. What takes time is to condense information into a few words that are direct, easy to understand, and still 100 percent accurate.

These days, many people describe these attributes as "user-friendly." A memo or presentation or speech is user-friendly if it conveys useful information in a relatively short period of time and is readable, relevant, and accurate.

Because people associate length with value — and because the business communications environment is often fast-paced — a common mistake is to create and distribute lengthy and poorly organized memos, Web sites, and other communications.

It's extremely important not to give in to these pressures. Our fellow employees are busy. They don't have time to wade through paragraphs of meaningless information or reread confusing sections. Carefully review your communications and include only the information readers really need. Reread the content and assure that it is well organized and can be delivered in as little space and take up as little of your audience's time as possible.

Before you add to a memo or Web page, ask yourself

if it's really necessary. Does it answer a vital who, what, when, where, or why question? Must recipients complete a requested action? Will it provide a real piece of business value? Or will it just take up space and time?

Just The Facts, Please

Stick to your topic and don't wander off on tangents. In a novel, for example, you wouldn't appreciate being told to feel a certain way about a character or situation. You want to reach that feeling on your own as a result of the story's elements, such as the character's actions, choices, or circumstances. For example,

No: Jane was a sad girl who always cried at movies. She was so pitiful; she had no friends at work or at school. The whole town felt sorry for her.

Yes: That Friday, Jane went to the old movie house on Pine for the 7 o'clock show. She went alone. No one there she knew. Got popcorn out of habit and sat on the right. Far enough from the speaker to keep her hearing, but far enough from the exit door to avoid the draft. In the dark she couldn't see the runs in her stockings, and it didn't matter that her coat was patched. No one else could see either. Didn't have to pretend she didn't notice the stares and sad whispers. In the dark, it was just her. And Scarlett, or Rhett. And a story that was happening to someone else.

Likewise in business communications, most employees don't appreciate being directed to think a certain way about the company or its direction and initiatives. Employees are intelligent, hard-working people. They can make up their own minds about corporate decisions and directions. But you must give them the facts and context to evaluate those activities for themselves. For example,

> **No:** A team charged to deploy a new software application to the sales force proposed the following key messages: *You'll love the new client management software the company is implementing next month! You'll find it's easy to use, and your customers will be happier too!*

The proposed key messages conveyed enthusiasm and optimism but didn't contain much real information. There was no way the recipients of the proposed messages would have been able to prepare for the new software or evaluate whether the messages were even close to being accurate.

> **Yes:** An alternative set of key messages might have looked like this: *You can expect to receive the new ABC Application in four weeks. Pilot results indicate that sales reps using the new tool to record customer complaints are speeding complaint resolution by 75 percent! Results also show that sales reps find the interface very user-friendly. Online education makes it possible to learn to use the application in only a few hours.*

The new set of messages reports facts from the pilot deployment that indicate not only that the audience will probably like the new application very much but also why the reception will probably be positive. This is a more credible set of messages than the first set.

Skip the Sizzle, but Keep the Vision

Let's face it: it's hard to make operational information compelling. Yet businesses must communicate new procedures or changed procedures that are boring at best and often detailed and confusing. Usually, too, these procedures are accompanied by value statements that connect them back to core company goals — such as continuous improvement or 100 percent customer satisfaction. Eventually, such communications sound more or less the same to recipients.

When that happens, teams scramble to add some sizzle to their communications and thus get recipients' attention — and risk miscommunication, overpromising, and audience skepticism. To avoid these problems, try to distinguish between the vision driving a project or initiative and the superfluous sizzle that will elicit only short-term attention.

Vision has to do with the company's long-term goals: delivering value to customers, partners, and employees. Sizzle has nothing to do real value; it has to do with perception. And if perception isn't backed by experience, it becomes a liability.

Instead of sizzle, add strong, fact-based statements that a project or initiative can live up to. Demonstrate proven benefits, track to solid corporate goals and values, and develop messaging strategies founded on delivering real information. If you must use sizzle, make it the last and least important element of your communications. Otherwise you are working on an internal advertising or promotional campaign, and that's entirely different from a communications program.

KISS, or Keep It Simple, Simply

There are many complexities in the world today. Take the time to communicate simply and accurately.

- Use simple words. This is especially important in organizations with diverse populations where English is not necessarily everyone's native language. It is also important in highly specialized environments where jargon and acronyms are common. We forget that not everyone knows what all the acronyms stand for. Using simple language and spelling out acronyms can be very helpful.

- Use simple, short sentences. Complex sentences can create more confusion than they're worth. Using simple noun-verb-object structures can help make a memo or Web page easy to understand.

- Keep the content short. In an era where many communications are reviewed on computer screens, it's increasingly important to keep content short and easily scannable. Break longer messages up with subheads or tables.

- Establish a regular messaging frequency. By issuing information about the company's pension plan once a quarter, for example, you will simplify the steps employees need to take to acquire new information on that topic.

- Sequence and parcel your messages. If you are working on a complex project with many implications and intersection points with various audiences and with other projects in the organizations, communicating those complexities can be very challenging. Introduce general concepts first and then more detailed and complex information as the audience's understanding of the program's messages grows.

- Stay in touch with your audience. Always remember that its priorities and concerns change with time. Keep your communications in step with them.

Active Voice - How Can You Tell?

Active versus passive voice: what is that and why does it matter in business communications? In business communications, we try to use forceful, direct language — that's the active voice, not the passive voice. There are two easy ways to recognize when you're using a passive construction: your sentence is probably longer than it needs to be and what would usually be the verb or object of the sentence in an active construction becomes the subject in the passive voice. The passive voice is a common mistake when we try to write formally. Here are some examples:

Passive: Use of the OK button will move you to the next screen in the application.
Active: Use the OK button to move to the next screen in the application.

Passive: Beginning 10 October, the South entrance is to be used by those people working weekends.
Active: Beginning 10 October, use the South entrance when working weekends.

Passive: Using the phone for personal calls is no longer allowed.

Active: Employees may no longer use the phone for personal calls.

Page Layout Tips

You don't need to be a graphic designer to create effective employee communications, but some simple design techniques can help make them more readable and engaging.

Less is More

One of the most common mistakes in communications is to put too much information on a page or in a memo. Most of us see what's on a page. Designers notice what is not on a page. They know to use empty space as deliberately as typography, artwork, and other design elements.

If you are writing the content, be brief and edit yourself. From a design point of view, consider how your paragraphs affect the flow of information and the page's scannability. Adjust the size of the typeface to increase readability.

Empty space is especially important on Web pages and in presentations. People can only absorb so much information at a time. Break out your concepts and include enough blank space around them to help readers absorb your points as you present them.

Typography and Type Effects

The less-is-more concept also applies to your typeface choices. Generally, sans serif fonts like Arial or Helvetica are easier to read, especially at large point sizes.

Serif fonts like Times New Roman are more common in formal environments. Avoid using too many different typefaces in the same communication. A typical rule of thumb is to use one typeface for the heading and subheads, and a closely related typeface for body copy.

Type effects refer to things such boldface, colored, or italicized type. Use them judiciously; avoid using too many different type effects in a single communication. A good rule of thumb for type effects is to use no more than three in a given memo or Web page.

Style and Consistency

Visual style and consistency refer to the repeated use of a certain typeface, for example, for all headings and subheadings. It can also refer to a consistent capitalization style for headings and subheadings.

For example, an all-initial caps style looks like this:
New Application Will Go Live Tomorrow

A sentence-style caps style looks like this:
New application will go live tomorrow

An all-caps style looks like this:
NEW APPLICATION WILL GO LIVE TOMORROW

Which style best suits your communications purpose?
Other visual style and consistency factors include page numbers, copyright symbols, and acronyms and abbreviations (versus using complete names).

Technology Factors

Resolution settings on computers will affect how your e-mail or other computer-delivered communications look, or even work, for recipients.

When you are gathering information about your project and your audience, be sure also to gather information about technical factors that must be considered when creating a communication.

A Few Good Resources

The following resources will come in handy if you are going to be creating communications for any length of time. They are also useful for normal business correspondence purposes.

- **Dictionary** — Splurge and buy one of the standard hardbound dictionaries such as *Merriam-Webster's Collegiate Dictionary: 10th Edition* (Merriam Webster) or *American Heritage Dictionary of the English Language: 4th Edition* (Houghton Mifflin Co.). Don't waste your money or time on the small, softcover dictionaries used by students. They don't have enough entries. Also, be aware that dictionaries differ. *Webster's*, for example, is a more traditional dictionary with a greater use of hyphenation. The *American Heritage* is more contemporary and includes words that *Webster's* doesn't yet recognize.

- **Thesaurus** — *Roget's Thesaurus* (Harper & Row) is the most common and, in my opinion, the best.

- **Strunk and White's** *Elements of Style* (MacMillan) — If you only buy one writing guide in your entire life, it should be this one. In the space of a very few pages, this little book has more good advice about writing than any other resource.

- ***Grammar Smart: A Guide to Perfect Usage*** (Princeton Review Series) — This book is great! It's easy to read, easy to understand, and full of examples that make complex English grammar rules easy to recognize and apply.

- **Notebook** — Every organization and project has its own unique language and preferred way of presenting information. To keep track of these elements, use a blank notebook divided into sections such as Capitalization styles, Word lists, Acronyms and meanings, etc.

Other good resources to include:

- ***The Elements of Editing*** (Arthur Plotnik, Macmillan)

- ***A Dictionary of Modern English Usage*** (H. W. Fowler, Oxford University Press)

- ***The Handbook of Non-Sexist Writing*** (Casey Miller)

Putting the Basics to Work

Okay, we have reviewed the basics, and now we're ready to put them to work to plan an employee communications program!

In this chapter, we'll look at what happens at the very beginning of a communications assignment, using two different scenarios. To illustrate how the basics work for small and large companies, we'll explore a scenario that targets a small, localized audience and another that affects a broader, more diverse population.

In the following two chapters, we'll continue with the same scenarios and move through the activities to finalize and execute a communications plan.

The chapters are designed so that the smaller project is first and the larger project is second. It's fine to focus first on one and skip the other. But it's probably a good idea to read them both through at least once to see for yourself how similarly this approach works for all sizes of audiences. Larger projects just involve asking more questions and asking them of more people.

Scenario 1: The Small Company

Company Profile

Sue and Henry Best own Best Realty Co., one of the most successful real estate companies in southern Colorado. The Bests are both brokers, and they own the company as equal partners. They employ eight realtors, three administrative assistants, and an office manager, who doubles as bookkeeper. All accounting and payroll services are outsourced. The company turned 16 years old in June, at the peak of a record-breaking 24 months.

The Business Problem

Best Realty manages an employee pension plan for its employees and offers full-time employees life, health, and disability insurance as part of its benefits program. It is a combination plan in which the company pays most of the premium costs and the employees contribute varying amounts, depending on the coverage options they select. Best Realty doesn't have enough employees to allow it to negotiate with insurers. The plan options it can buy are standardized based on state-defined requirements and on the number of insured in their small group.

Shortly after the company's Sweet Sixteen party in June, the Bests learned that insurance costs would increase 25 percent in October and that pension plan investments for the period January through June fell in value by 40 percent. Additionally, while new-home sales in southern Colorado were still coming in at a good clip, sales of existing homes had reached a plateau and industry analysts expected them to drop by 20 percent over the next two to three months.

The Bests recognized that several actions were now required. First, they must let their employees know about the upcoming insurance increases as well as the drop in value of the pension plan. Second, they must reduce staff by two realtors and one administrative assistant by the end of September. And third, they must investigate other insurance and investment management options.

The Communication Assignment

The Bests have asked us to design a program to communicate this information to the employees. It should include the immediate changes as well as information about longer-term actions.

The existing communications structure in Best Realty is informal. The company holds "all-hands" meetings every month around the 15th. The August gathering is always an end-of-summer picnic for employees and families.

Get Started!

The first thing to do is make a list of what we need to do — how will we approach this assignment?

1. Define our objectives, guiding principles, and requirements by answering the Five Ws. Use this information to draft a plan.

2. Identify the types of information required and who can provide each. These sources will be our subject matter experts (SMEs).

3. Identify what skills are required to execute the draft plan. For example, do we need to translate from English to Spanish? Or build and use an electronic mailing list? If we're going to print something, we might need graphic design skills, and so on. At this point, we assess whether we have all the skills and the time to use them in this project. We might need to bring in other people with the right skills. If we do add people to our team, we will want to ensure that they all understand their roles and responsibilities.

4. Finally, we should take the time now to define the steps we'll use to complete each major set of activities in the plan, which might include any or all of the following: develop the communication, deploy or launch it, measure its effectiveness, and consider what worked and what didn't and use that to improve the rest of the plan.

1. Answer the Five Ws

a. Who are the audiences for this communications program, and what are their characteristics?

To start, we'll note all the details about the audiences that we already know in an audience assessment matrix. Remember that you can use any format you want to — just be sure to cover all the bases in terms of the questions you ask and the information you collect. (See Figure 8.)

After we complete the matrix, it's easy to see that we already know a lot about these audiences. After all, we work with them and to a certain extent we are friends.

However, there are a few things we don't know: historical factors that we should consider, specific timing aspects, and any other objectives or tactics that might come into play. These might be uncovered as we progress through these first steps so we will wait to ask Sue and Henry any more questions for the time being. If we had more gaps, we might consider getting that information now rather than waiting.

Audience Assessment Summary Matrix

	Realtors	Administrative Staff
Description	8 full-time realtors; 5 men and 3 women	3 administrative assts. and 1 office manager/supervisor
Characteristics		
Language	English	English and Spanish
Cultural factors	All U.S. citizens, one naturalized	All U.S. citizens, 2 naturalized from Mexico
Line of business factors	Mostly residential sales; 2 realtors studying for broker licenses	1 is studying for realtor's license; the 2 Mexican-born staff serve as translators with Spanish-speaking customers
Historical factors		Admin tasks are least liked by realtors
Information needs	Need to know about pension plan and insurance cost changes, and layoff plans	Need to know about pension plan and insurance cost changes, and layoff plans
Media preferences	Highly mobile group; uses Palm and cell phones, irregular use of e-mail	Adept with e-mail
Messenger preferences	All messages should come from Sue and Henry	All messages should come from Sue and Henry with some funneled through office manager/ supervisor
Message preferences	Face-to-face with handouts	Face-to-face with hand outs
Alternate channels	none	none
Key objective of communication	To give info and to set expectations given softening business environment	To give info and to set expectations given softening business environment
Possible tactics for key objective	Keep tone professional yet humanistic and real; stick to the the facts; can company offer placement support?	Keep tone professional yet humanistic and real; stick to the the facts; can company offer placement support?
Known challenges	Face-to-face mtgs are hard to coordinate with schedules; some will hear news secondhand	Availability is not such a problem with this group
Key milestones and messaging needs		
Other objectives and tactics		

Figure 8

b. What do we need to know about this situation in order to communicate with employees about how it affects them?

We need to know in general what the topics are and who is qualified to deliver information about them. We should know any timing requirements established by corporate policy or legal mandate. We should know if there are vendors involved or other players who should have a voice and presence. And we should have a general idea of what important milestones exist, as well as any other factors that might influence our planning. (See figure 9)

Information Outline	
Best Realty	
Topics to be communicated	Benefits changes and layoffs
Who should deliver messages?	Sue and Henry to realtors and office manager; perhaps OM to administrate?
When must 1st communication occur?	No later than 31 August re: pension fund
Vendors involved and their role(s)	Insurance agency and investment agency fund manager (consider having these reps come speak)
Next key milestones	Must notify employees about insurance costs and 30-day notice for layoffs by 30 September
	Must report back to employees about pension fund investment change plans no later than 31 October (Would be good to report on insurance options at the same time)
Other issues to consider	How does this connect – or should it – with the end of summer picnic on 15 August? In last two years, we've reported the fund performance at this picnic. However, it was good news then.

Figure 9

c. Then, we need to begin to document the specific pieces of information that need to be delivered — and how they vary, if at all, by audience.

These points will become key messages in the communications and will come out of a closer inquiry about the project: the when, where, and why questions. (Figure 10)

Key Messages	Best Realty	The Realtors	The Staff
When people are laid off, what will change for the employees that remain?	Our commitment to customers and staff remain unchanged.	No changes to terms of employment contract other than those required by the new insurance contracts.	No expected change to hrs, but shared work will change since fewer people will be supporting realtors
			At least one Spanish-speaking employee will remain to support Spanish customers with translation services
Will there be outplacement support for laid-off workers?		Laid-off realtors will receive a compensation pkg. consistent with their employment contract. No other services provided	Laid-off support staff will receive 30 days' severance and 30 days' placement assistance
What effort is the company making to improve the invest-ment services of the pension plan?	Will need to outline this info and provide timeline for when info will be available		
What effort is the company making to improve employees' insurance options?	Will need to outline this info and provide timeline for when info will be available		

Figure 10

d. At the end of our *Who, What, When, Where, Why* inquiry, we should have a complete audience analysis in hand.

In this case, we added the following information to our audience assessment from 1.a.:

Historical factors	First and only layoffs in this company	Admin tasks are least liked by realtors; significant backlogs customer dissatisfaction have built up at different times.

and

Key milestones and messaging needs	Must communicate pension performance within the month of July; must advise re: insurance cost changes before 31 August; must allow 30 days notice for any layoffs and those layoffs must be in effect no later than 30 Sept.	Same requirements

e. We should also have the following items drafted:

- A preliminary communication plan (Figure 11)

Draft Plan

Launch Date	Deliverable	Audience	Key Message	Media	Sender/speaker
1 Aug	Company picnic reminder	All employees	Remind them to set date aside and come for fun!	Memo/ bulletin board posting	Sue and Henry
14 Aug	Pension plan performance	All full-time employees	Report perform-ance 1H of year, actions company is taking and when employees will be advised of changes or decisions they must make	Memo	Sue, as fund administrator; consider including fund agent name and contact info so people can contact fund directly
15 Aug	Company picnic	All employees and families	No business messages at all	Face-to-face	Sue and Henry
15 Sept	Insurance rate increases	All full-time employees	Tell what the new insurance costs will be & effective date; report actions co. is taking to improve cover-age options	Part of Sept. all-hands meeting; provide handout	Henry. See if fund agent can be present to answer questions
15 Sept	Pension plan status	All full-time employees	Report co. decision re: improving fund performance	Part of Sept. all-hands meeting; provide handout	Sue. See if fund agent can be present to answer questions
15 Sept	Layoffs	All full-time employees	Explain that lay-offs are due to economic climate; difficult decision but required	Part of Sept. all-hands meeting	Sue and Henry
30 Sept	Layoffs	Those being laid off	Confidential and personal dismissal with thanks and severances as per role in company	Face-to-face with escort to collect belong-ings and depart premises	

Figure 11

- Communication objectives
  - ✠ Communicate sensitive and negative financial and resource-related information to employees in a realistic and nonthreatening fashion.
  - ✠ Ensure that employees receive accurate and fact-based details regarding financial and resource-related decisions.
  - ✠ Ensure that employee options and decision opportunities are clearly stated and profiled.
- Guiding principles
  - ✠ Business owners will deliver all financial and resource-related messages to employees.
  - ✠ Third-party experts will be available to answer questions from employees directly if possible.
  - ✠ Information will be communicated openly and in a timely fashion; however, personal details will be held strictly confidential.

2. What additional information do we need, and who can provide it?

Basically, the information we need to complete our plan and first drafts is probably going to come from Sue or Henry and be supplemented by the insurance agent and the pension fund manager. We would want to take the following steps to move forward:

a. **Meet with Sue and Henry to validate the draft plan** and identify who we should speak with to get the rest of the information we need.

b. **Find out when information should be available** and compare those dates with the date we need it by to create and finalize the communication.

c. **Adjust our plan based on this input.**

3. Assess what skills are required to execute this plan and what skills are available. Do we need help?

In this case, we need interview skills to collect the information and then writing and basic page-layout skills. But that's about it. All the employees speak and read English, so we don't need any translation work. We don't need any graphic design skills because the communications are text-based and low-key. They don't involve any posters or other strong visual presentations. We don't need any electronic distribution help, because all the communications will be executed using hard copy in face-to-face meetings. And the situation has a beginning, middle, and end, so there are no long-term needs that might have warranted a small team's ongoing focus. As a result, we don't need to set up a team or define roles and responsibilities.

4. What steps will we take to execute the plan?

For this situation, the most important steps are to develop the content and ensure that it's accurate. Sue and Henry will distribute the communications once they're done. No formal measurement or lessons learned steps are probably necessary, though we might suggest that Best Realty establish a formal communications process based on the steps we've used here.

a. The review cycle for each communication should include Sue and Henry. It might also include the insurance agent and fund manager at different points, to ensure the facts about these programs are accurate.

We want to make sure that Sue, Henry, and the vendors understand what we need from them during the review cycle. We don't need them, for example, to rewrite the communication — unless they really want to. We do need them to point out content that is inaccurate or confusing. Perhaps the information in a memo or a presentation is in the wrong sequence, for example. And we need Sue or Henry, since their names will be at the bottom of the memos, to help us refine the wording so that it sounds like them.

We also need them to understand how much time they have to review the content and give us their feedback. The schedule might be full of time or quite tight.

We also want them to understand and agree with our approach up front. If we aren't successful on this count, we will run into problems when we actually sit down to create the memo or presentation — and that will take time to resolve when we might not have any extra time at all!

b. We need to be sure that Sue and Henry understand their responsibility to distribute the communications once they're final. We will give them the final content, but they will be responsible for ensuring the right number of copies and handouts are available at the meetings. Of course, in a small company, we'd probably help out here, too, but maybe not.

c. We should also talk with Sue and Henry about how they want to receive questions or feedback from employees about these communications and their content. Public questions and answers might be appropriate for the all-hands meetings, but some people might not want to ask all their questions in that setting. Will Sue or Henry be available at other times to answer these questions? This information also needs to be communicated to the employees.

d. Finally, we want to arrange with Sue and Henry to monitor the communications events to ensure that the messages are working as anticipated and make corrections if they aren't. In a small company, we'd probably be there as a fellow employee. But again, maybe not.

And that's it for Best Realty for this chapter. In the next chapter, we'll take the objectives, the draft plan, and some of our closing questions and move forward to finalize the plan and key messages.

If you want to skip ahead and follow Best Realty through to the end, go ahead. Do come back, at some point, and read through the other scenario. You'll find that there are actually few differences between small and large companies when it comes to putting communications basics to work.

Scenario 2: The Larger Company

Company profile

Fine Family Furniture is a leading retail furniture outlet in the Rocky Mountain region. The company operates 20 stores, 3 warehousing units, a call center, and a fleet of 50 delivery vehicles in 10 Western states. The company employs 350-400 salespeople, 150 administrative and finance people, and 250 mostly part-time warehouse and transportation staff. The executive headquarters is in Phoenix, with the company's operational headquarters located in Salt Lake City and the Human Resources department is in Denver.)

Fine Family Furniture is thirty years old. It was started by Doug Jimson in 1973. Jimson's grandson,

Todd, is now CEO, with granddaughter, Celia, as VP, Finance. The company is privately held, though there has been increasing interest in going public and using that capital to expand into new markets in the U.S.

The Business Problem

The Rocky Mountain region has been fast-growing for the last decade. During that time, Fine Family improved its warehousing and transportation divisions and recently decided to upgrade its inventory control system and customer database and credit processing systems.

The systems are almost ready to deploy, and the team is preparing the communications to support introduction of the new technology. There are a number of issues with the rollout, including the following:

- Salespeople now don't use any computer systems. Instead, they rely on administrative support to call up customer records and run credit checks.

- For inventory checks, salespeople call the warehouses directly. Warehouse staff must physically check availability and then call the salesperson back. Some inquiries take days to answer since the salesperson must call three different warehouses, and the warehouses in turn are trying to respond to inquiries from all 300 salespeople, for multiple customers.

- One of the ways the company has managed this situation in the past has been to keep a very large inventory available in each retail location. However, this strategy has not been able to keep pace with current demand in several locations experiencing high growth.

- Part of the rollout of the new technology includes education for all staff on use of the new system, which people will have to complete partially on company time and partially on their own time.

- Another aspect is the introduction of computer kiosks throughout the retail locations. Customers will be able to check stock availability on the spot if a salesperson is not available. Access to sensitive information, such as vendor pricing, will only be accessible at certain workstations and with appropriate login credentials.

The company's employee communications programs are managed by the HR department in Denver. The current process calls for reviews by senior HR personnel only and a segmented approach by employee job function and location.

The last time Fine Family Furniture implemented a company-wide training program or system upgrade was five years ago when the travel voucher program was revamped. At that time, there were only 350-400 employees and 14 retail locations. Additionally, most employees were not expected to enter travel transactions into the system themselves but route all vouchers through their managers to the travel department for processing.

The current implementation is a radical change for this company, made necessary by changing market conditions and consumers' increasingly sophisticated expectations. While many staff are looking forward to the new systems, many are not.

Not surprisingly, the cost of this new system, including hardware, software, and training, is high. The management team expects a lot in return, and the project team is under a lot of scrutiny.

The Communication Assignment

The VP of HR has asked us to join the project team as communication specialists to support the rollout of the new system throughout the company. We will be responsible to the project leader for all required communications and will be expected to execute communications activities according to the company's existing process. We'll also report on the project's status to our current manager in HR on a weekly basis.

Get Started!

As you can see, this is quite a different scenario than the preceding exercise. There are more people involved; the topic has to do with technology as opposed to resource or benefits programs; and the audiences are spread out across 10 states in a multiplicity of job roles. But again, the first thing to do is to understand what it is that we need to do — how will we approach this assignment?

We know that there is an existing communications process in Fine Family Furniture. However that process is constructed, it must cover the same basic activities that we listed in the Best Realty scenario:

1. Define the objectives, guiding principles, and requirements by answering the Five Ws. Use this information to draft a plan.

2. Identify the types of information required and who can provide them. These sources will be our subject matter experts.

3. Identify what skills are required to execute the draft plan, including translation, graphic design, electronic list management, audience or technical expertise, etc. Determine who we need to add to our team, and ensure that everyone understands their part by defining the roles and responsibilities.

4. Define the steps we'll use to complete each major set of activities in the plan, including develop the communication, deploy or launch it, measure its effectiveness, and then consider what worked and what didn't and use that to improve the rest of the plan.

1. Answer the Five Ws

a. Who are the audiences for this communications program, and what are their characteristics?

You'll notice that there are several blank areas left on the form. (Figure 12) That's okay.

Audience Assessment Summary Matrix

	Senior Execs.	Storage & Faculty Mgrs.	Salespeople	Admin. Staff	Warehouse & Transportation
Description	HQ execs. not line execs	Approx. 60; all locations	Approx. 375; all locations; mostly full-time	Approx. 150; all locations	Approx. 250; all locations; PT & shift labor
Characteristics					
Language	English	English and Spanish			
Cultural factors	All U.S. citizens	Most U.S. citizens	Most U.S. citizens, many Mexican-Americans		
Line of bus. factors	N/A	Most store hours: 8 a.m. - 9 p.m. M-Sat; shifts are 8 hours long. Current training plans are to close for one Tuesday-Wednesday period to conduct education sessions for all facility staff. Follow-up sessions TBD.			Similar approach as for stores; schedule follow-up sessions since some drivers out of town
Historical factors					
Information needs					
Media preferences	In-person mtgs. are most common; minimal use of e-mail; mobile, hard to schedule	e-mail and hard-copy memos from senior mgmt., face-to-face and hard-copy memos with store staff	Face-to-face and hard-copy memos; very little use of e-mail though all have it	Use e-mail the most but many have dedicated worksta-tions	Hard-copy memos and face-to-face meetings
Messenger preferences	Exec. sponsor is VP Finance, a peer	Senior exec. who acts as direct supervisor is strongest	Store manager		Facility or transportation manager
Message preferences	Short	Short/reusable	Short & immedi-ately applicable	Short	Relevance to circumstances
Alt. channels	none				
Other matrix items as needed					

Figure 12

The point is not to fill in 100 percent of the blanks but to take stock first of what you know and then identify what else you need to find out. Let's keep going.

b. What do we need to know about this situation in order to communicate with employees about how it affects them?

Project Outline	
Fine Family Furniture	
Project name	Need to find out if project has a name or logo yet.
Describe project	I/T project to install new workstations for use by all employees; new workstations will contain new software that will allow for better inventory control and customer credit profiling.
Executive sponsor(s)	VP Finance
Who should deliver messages	VP Finance to senior execs; Departmental senior exec to store and facility managers; store and facility managers to location employees, all roles
Overall start date and duration	Deployment starts in Phoenix in March and should end in Montana in late May.
Vendors involved/roles	Don't think this matters for us.
Relationship to market	This will improve the company's ability to service our customers. We'll be able to answer availability questions more quickly and accurately, as well as conduct immediate credit checks for customers interested in making purchases.
Project objectives	Improve inventory control data collection and information sharing so employees have information they need in real-time. Decrease amount of time wasted by managing this information manually and communicating it one request at a time. Improve customer data and credit information records so credit checks can be executed in real-time with minimal customer inconvenience.
Productivity improvement measure and revenue projections are detailed within each division	Not available.
Total audience affected	All part-time and full-time employees.
How will audiences be affected?	All will have to be educated on new system. All will have access to a workstation; many will now have dedicated workstations.
How will customers be affected?	Will have direct access to credit line & inventory info by using computer kiosks in showrooms to check availability. Plans for same services via Web are in process; not available until March.
When must 1st communication occur?	Begin communications 4 weeks prior to education start date in each location.
Will project require store or facility closure?	Yes. All stores and warehouse facilities will close for a Tuesday-Wednesday period to complete training sessions.
Will project require any personal time investment?	Training will probably require personal time investment but extent is not yet known.
Other issues to consider	None currently known.

Figure 13

Figure 13 shows a good start at collecting project-level detail. We know quite a bit about this project in a very short time frame. We also know we'll have to focus more closely on some key areas later on. For example, we know everyone will be taught about the new systems, but we don't know what the schedule is or what we need to tell our different audiences. We also don't know if the company has named the project internally — and if they have, then it's a safe guess that a lot of employees, like us, are not aware of it. Another important set of facts that we'll need to understand much more clearly as we get closer to deployment is this one involving employees' personal time. Just what will be required of them, anyway?

It's important to remember too, that we are responsible for communications. We are not responsible for resolving issues related to the project — unless we also work in areas in addition to communications. It's easy to forget that distinction in the heat of a project.

c. Next, we must begin to document the specific pieces of information that need to be delivered — and how they vary, if at all, by audience. These points will become key messages in the communications and come out of a closer inquiry about the project: the when, where, and why questions.

The message matrix (Figure 14) on page 128 illustrates how the levels of detail will increase as we learn more about the project. The other useful feature of key messages and key message families is that we can collect, in advance, a good percentage of the wording that we will actually end up using! That gives us more time to get approvals from executives and others involved in the content review cycle. And the more items that everyone agrees on in advance, the better because that will speed the actual development time later.

Message Matrix Cross-reference which messages apply to which audiences and if modification is required	Senior Execs	Store & Facility	Sales Mgrs.	Admin. Staff	Warehouse & Transport
Business rationale					
FFF spends an estimated 30,000 personnel hours per year just answering basic inventory control questions. This system will cut that expense by 80 percent.	X	X	X		X
FFF salespeople & warehouse staff could service an estimated $2.5 million in sales if they didn't spend so much time answering inventory control questions. That comes to an estimated wage increase of 30 percent per salesperson and warehouse employee.	X	X	X		X
We lose too many sales because of the time it takes to complete initial credit checks. The new system will speed that step by 35 percent. Customer will even be able to check their own credit.	X	X	X	X	
Implementation schedule					
The project team has been working for nearly a year to define system requirements, create code and conduct tests.	X	X			
Beginning in March, employees in the Phoenix area will be trained on the new system and have hardware installed in showroom and warehouse locations. Productive use of the system scheduled for 7 March.	X	X	X, selective	X, selective	X, selective
The deployment will then move to every FFF store in Arizona. Other states will follow in a phased deployment that will complete in early May. Exact details for your store or warehouse location will be communicated to your managers as they are finalized.	X	X	X, selective	X, selective	X, selective
We need to know the current plan and order of states.	X	X	X	X	X
Education schedule					
Every FFF employee will be trained to use the new system. Training will be delivered in classroom settings at your store or warehouse on a Tuesday-Wednesday prior to implementation.	X	X	X	X	X
Every employee will also be expected to prepare for the new system by completing at-home studies prior to the formal training. Full details will be given to your manager as the deployment for your location nears.	X	X	X	X	X
If you have no computer experience at all, don't worry! The education that you will receive will include basic computer skills.	X	X	X	X	X
Benefits					
The most important benefit of this new system is that all our stores and warehouses will now be able to "talk" with each other. Employees at any location will be able to quickly and accurately look up model availability with a few keystrokes.	X	X	X	X	X
Customers will also be able to access availability information in a twinkling.	X	X	X		
The other principal benefit is that employees can quickly run credit checks for customers considering a purchase. This will tell you the amount of credit the customer can expect to receive from FFF, and you can target your selling efforts accordingly.	X	X	X	X	
Because employees will have access to better information more easily, they will be able to respond to customers more quickly and effectively, which will make customers happier and also give employees more opportunities to improve their own revenue.		X	X		

Figure 14

d. At the end of our *Who, What, When, Where, Why* inquiry, we should be able to deliver two items: A complete audience analysis and a preliminary communication plan.

So, we are able to add the following items to our audience assessment from our *What* questions (Figure 15a):

Historical factors	Most extensive such project ever for this company. Little prior reliance on computerization; some employees are grumbling.	
Information needs	Will need to be trained also, as all management reports will reside in the new system.	All employees must be educated on new system and related hardware.

Figure 15a

And add this information as a result of our *When, Where,* and *Why* questions (Figures 15b and 15c):

Key objective of communication	Ensure senior executives understand the project, its importance to the business and their particular areas of responsibility. Ensure they can model desired behavior and use the new technology to manage business and make decisions.	Ensure managers understand importance of new technology and how they can use it to manage their business. Ensure they understand how important it is for them to model desired new behavior for employees.	Help employees understand what they must do to be able to use the new technology effectively. Encourage active participation.
Possible tactics for key objective	Give executives short soundbites of information so they can appear knowledgeable to employees and reinforce key messages about project.	Keep tone of communications professional yet humanistic; keep channels very open and candid. Ensure this group can answer employee questions and reinforce both strategic and tactical.	Keep tone of communications professional yet humanistic; set realistic expectations; and demonstrate how this technology will improve employees' work days; stick to the facts.

Figure 15b

Known challenges	This group isn't used to accessing a system to pull information they need; this will be an entirely new behavior, yet the group is committed to making the change.	Members of this group reflect the silo environment the company is seeking to integrate by introducing this technology; old behavior patterns that have worked well for these people will not change quickly.	Employees are expected to be generally enthusiastic about new technology although direct supervisor modeling will influence attitudes.
Key milestones and messaging needs	Technology deployment starts in Phoenix in March and is scheduled to end in Montana in late May. Communications will start roughly 4 weeks prior to deployment of education for each location based on actual deployment schedule.		

Figure 15c

e. By this time, we should also have drafts of the following:

- A preliminary communications plan (Figure 16)

Draft Plan

Launch date	Deliverable	Audience	Key Message	Media	Sender/speaker
30 days prior to education	Executive memo	Senior execs and store facility managers	Set context for project; announce when education and deployment will happen for each state facility; state required participation levels, time commitments, staffing and logistical requirements; contact information for further details; include brochure and general information messages managers can use with staff	E-mail, hard copy memo, suggested staff-directed memos and brochures (possible poster in lunchroom)	VP Finance
14 days prior to education	Action memo	All location employees	Set context for project, confirm location's education and deployment schedules; reaffirm mandatory attendance at education and other expectations of employees; deliver prerequisite materials for self-study activities on employees' own time	Hard-copy memo with attached self-study, calendar, and checklist to confirm employee is ready.	VP Finance sends package to location manager for use and distribution under own signature
3 days prior to education	Reminder memo	All location employees	Reminder of scheduled education and deployment activities, employee required actions, etc.	Hard-copy memo and possible signs for bulletin boards	Send directly to location manager to distribute to employees
3 days after productive use begins	Thank you memo and status report	All location employees	Thank employees for making the transition work well; report on how well the store did in terms of employee participation in training and deployment activities (will there be a contest and prize?)	Hard-copy memo and bulletin board announcement; use in an all-hands setting	Location manager issues to location employees using template and message points provided
14 days after productive use begins	Interim status report	Senior execs and location managers	Report on early usage statistics; pinpoint any early user or behavioral problems and related corrective action; transition location to be part of general monthly project status report beginning at month-end	E-mail and hard-copy version for use only by executives and location management	Location manager sends
30 days after productive use begins; then ongoing	Monthly system status report	Senior execs and location managers	Report usage statistics at location or state levels; pinpoint user and behavior problems; report on system malfunctions and corrective actions taken or in process; identify required user corrective actions ; report on earned ROI.	E-mail and hard copy version for use only by executives and location management	VP Finance sends

Figure 16

- Communication objectives
  - ✠ Communicate actions required of locations and employees to receive the new inventory control and customer credit inquiry system.
  - ✠ Reinforce key corporate messages about project and benefits expected.
  - ✠ Help drive 100 percent participation on the part of all employees and locations in education and deployment-related activities.
- Guiding principles:
  - ✠ Ask local managers to rally employees and take personal responsibility for success of education and deployment.
  - ✠ Provide accurate information concerning required actions.
  - ✠ Provide succinct and accurate details about success of implementation and corrective actions, immediately before and after deployment.
  - ✠ Disrupt normal business communications as little as possible.

2. What additional information do we need, and who can provide it?

For an audience of this size and diversity, we will probably need to speak with employees on the project team who are familiar with specific audience segments and with how the new system will affect those segments. At the very least, we will want to interview them about the project and the user segment they represent. We will also want to arrange for them to review the draft communications later in the process to ensure we've captured the details correctly.

We will also need to ensure that our package approach works with the company's existing message distribution system. Again, HR should be able to compile lists of senior executives and location managers for electronic mail purposes as well as hard-copy mail. But that must be confirmed and scheduled. Then, too, we'll have to ensure that the bundle of communication templates for each location manager is easy to use. So we will probably want to arrange to test the package at the same time the education is tested, prior to beginning the rollout. There might be requirements concerning posters that will affect printing and distribution plans, too.

It would be a good idea to work closely with the education team since so much of the communications activity actually supports education. We want to stay on top of any changes to this schedule or to the deployment schedule, in general.

3. Assess what skills are required to execute this plan and what skills are available. Do we need help?

Because there might be a poster as part of this communications package, we will want to add a graphic designer to our team. He or she might participate throughout the entire project or just for a short period, to create the poster visual and printing specifications.

It's hard to tell so far, but we might need some translation skills also. It might be important to have information available in English and Spanish, particularly for locations in the Southwest. The HR department has probably already faced this problem, and should be able to give us an answer very easily.

In this size of a company and effort, it's possible that we will be the only communications resource for this project and that we won't set up a communications subteam. In that case, we will have to manage the different elements independently and bring in the experts we need, such as a graphic designer, when we need them.

4. What steps will we take to execute the plan?

In this situation, there are more people involved in the project, the information to be conveyed, and the methods that will be employed to convey it. For that reason, it's wise to spend a little more time documenting the processes that we'll use and confirming with other players what we expect them to do. To start, we must:

a. Review the draft plan, objectives, and guiding principles with our manager and with the VP, Finance.

b. Define the content review process and confirm it with our manager and the VP, Finance.

c. Define and validate the distribution sequence with our manager and ensure that a staff person is assigned.

d. Ensure that project manager adds a communications test to the project plan, simultaneous with the education test activities.

e. Define the success criteria and how they will be measured.

That's it for Fine Family Furniture. If you are reading each scenario through from start to finish, then you will want to move on to the next chapter. But be sure you come back and read the other scenario to see how similar the communications activities are, regardless of the company's size or even the topics being discussed.

At some point too, you can return to this chapter and test yourself or use the chapter to begin work on a communications project in your own organization. You are welcome to use or modify any of the forms in this book to put the basics to work anytime. Just follow these four key points:

1. Answer the Five Ws and create a preliminary communications plan.

2. What additional information do I need, and who can provide it?

3. Assess what skills are required to complete this plan and what skills are available. Do I need help?

4. What steps will I take to execute the plan?

Fleshing Out the Plan

In the previous chapter, we went over the activities that happen at the very beginning of a communications assignment, using two different scenarios: a small company needing to communicate some resource actions; and a larger, more diverse company preparing to deploy a new IT system. In this chapter, we'll use this preliminary work to construct final communications plans for each scenario. In the next chapter, we'll put those plans to work.

As before, the smaller project comes first and the larger project follows. You can choose to read one at a time and skip the other one. Or you can read through both scenarios and then take what applies to your situation and modify it for your use.

Scenario 1: Best Realty

Where We Left Off

We accomplished a lot in the preceding chapter.

• Completed an audience analysis and outline of the project, including key messages for each audience.

• Identified the types of detailed information we need to include in the communications and who will help us get that information.

• Identified the skills we need to produce the communications and who has those skills.

• Defined our communication objectives and guiding principles.

• Produced a preliminary plan detailing the proposed communications and the primary audience, media, and timing for each.

Where We're Headed Next

We closed the Best Realty section of the last chapter with a list of four sets of activities:

• The review cycle used to develop communications

• The distribution responsibilities once a communication is complete

- The feedback cycle that should be embedded in the communication

- The measurement or assessment cycle to note whether the communications are having the desired effect.

We discussed these activities in the last chapter, but we didn't document the steps that comprise them. We will start by doing that, and then we will return to the preliminary communications plan of the last chapter and we will work that into a detailed plan, complete with tasks, timelines, milestones, a critical path, and resources.

A Word About Process

What is a *business process*? Unless you have worked in a large company, you may never have heard this term. A business process is a collection of steps employees take to complete a business activity.

The concept is actually very simple: to increase consistency and efficiency in all parts of a company. The expected results include reducing costs and increasing productivity and also improving quality.

So let's define the processes we will use to create, distribute, obtain feedback about, and measure communications. Our processes will simply be lists of steps that we should take to keep our communications program moving forward.

Does this sound like a lot of busywork? There are two advantages to taking the time to do it:

1. You will have clear instructions and expectations

to communicate to your staff and teammates. This lets you delegate tasks more effectively and helps reduce the number of errors made by relying on memory and guesswork.

2. You will create a repeatable set of steps that can be reused at any time by you, your team, and other members of your company, which will give you a foundation on which to act and also improve over time.

What Processes Will We Define and Use?

There are two basic activities that must happen for every communication.

1. Develop, review, and finalize the communication. This process guides you and your teammates through the draft, review, and edit steps.

Each communication program is different, and each set of reviewers is also often different. Many people have never acted as reviewers or subject matter experts in a communication program. Documenting these steps can be helpful to everybody to ensure they understand their role in the process. (See Figure 17.) For example, reviewers should each get their comments back to you within no more than one business day, according to the process we've defined. They should also know they need only give us their comments to correct or clarify content. They are not expected to rewrite the communication.

The Development Process and Review Cycle			
#	Process step	Description of Activity	Elapsed
1	Draft communication	Construct the first draft of the communication, including graphic elements if available.	Can vary. Allow 1 week.
2	Review draft with subject matter experts (SMEs)	Circulate the first draft for review by each SME in the review cycle. For Best Realty, this will be: 1. Sue or Henry 2. Insurance agent or financial fund manager 3. Sue's secretary, Mary, as a second pair of editorial eyes	Allow 1 business day for each
3	Receive comments and changes	1. Consolidate all the feedback and review it. 2. If there is conflicting feedback, review it with Sue to resolve. 3. If additional information is needed, get that information. 4. If you don't know who has that information, ask Sue for direction.	Can vary. General estimate is 2 business days.
4	Complete second draft of communication	Review first draft based on feedback and direction received.	Can vary. Allow 2 business days.
5	Review second draft w/ SMEs	Same as step 2.	1 bus. day for each
6	Receive comments	Same as step 3.	Can vary. Allow 2 business days.
7	Finalize communication	1. Feedback and comments on the 2nd draft should be minimal unless there is a direction change from the sponsor or a significant information change from a SME. 2. If there is limited feedback or changes to the 2nd draft, do a final edit and release as final to Mary to distribute. 3. If there is still a significant change by the end of the 2nd draft's review, then you might need to create and circulate a 3rd draft for review, and so on until feedback indicates acceptance.	Can vary. General estimate is 1 business day unless further drafts and reviews are required.

Figure 17

2. Distribute the communication.

This is a critical and often overlooked step. You can create a fantastic communication, but if you can't get it to the people who need to receive it, then it makes absolutely no difference at all. See Figure 18 on page 140.

We've talked about this challenge briefly in earlier chapters, and this is where you must iron out the details surrounding distribution. Who will be responsible for the distribution lists? Who will be responsible for actually distributing the communication as a handout or as an e-mail? How much time do these people need to complete their activities, such as making copies if the communication is a handout. And in larger companies, you will want to understand the degree of segmentation that's possible and efficient. For Best Realty, everyone in the company

The Distribution Process		
For handouts	**Description of activity**	**Elapsed time**
1 Photocopy final communication	Mary will print out the communication on the appropriate letterhead and arrange to have 25 copies made, front and back if communication is longer than one page.	Allow 1 business day for up to 10 pages. Allow 2 days for longer documents.
2 Distribute communication at meetings	Mary will ensure the copies are available to Sue and Henry to distribute. Exact calendar dates TBD.	1 business day for each.
For e-mail		
1 Convert communication to e-mail	Mary will convert the communication to an e-mail format.	Can vary. Allow 1 business day.
2 Distribute e-mail from appropriate sender	Mary will coordinate release of e-mail from either Sue or Henry, depending on subject.	Varies. Allow 1 business day.
Logistics of meetings		
1 Reserve meeting room	Mary will reserve the meeting room.	1 business day.
2 Ensure equipment and refreshments are available	Mary will arrange for equipment, which includes attendee and presenter seating, tables if needed, overhead or projector, TV and video if needed, pads and pencils, etc. Refreshments can be ordered from All-in-One Bakery and charged to Best Realty's corporate account. Amount cannot exceed $50 per meeting.	Can vary. General estimate is 1 business day.

Figure 18

will be receiving the same messages, so segmentation is not an issue or a work item to worry about.

Two other activities sometimes also happen:

3. Create opportunities for end-user feedback.
This process will not be part of every communication program, though many experts believe it should be.

Best Realty, in our example, has chosen to include opportunities for feedback in this series of communications. That means someone must be assigned to receive and respond to it. They will also track and report on how much feedback is received and its nature. This information will be used in the measurement process, and it will also help the management team, Sue and Henry, gauge the morale and concerns of their employees. (Figure 19)

The Feedback Process			
#	Process Step	Description of Activity	Elapsed
1	Feedback resource	All communications activities must have a person assigned to receive and respond to employee feedback and questions. For this program in Best Realty, the resource will be Henry's assistant, Jack.	N/A
2	Feedback information	Jack's contact information must be included in all the communications.	N/A
3	Feedback monitoring	Jack will monitor his in-box daily for any employee feedback or questions related to these communications.	N/A
4	Feedback response	1. Jack will respond to any employee feedback or questions within one business day of the feedback. 2. If Jack cannot answer the question himself, he will engage the appropriate SME for assistance. 3. If a complete answer cannot be obtained and communicated within one business day, Jack will still respond to the employee and tell him or her when a complete answer can be expected.	1 business day
5	Feedback documentation	1. Jack will document all the feedback and questions received, as well as the answers supplied. 2. Jack will review this material with the communications team at regular intervals: daily or weekly, depending on volume.	Daily or weekly, depending on volume
6	Use of feedback to direct future activities	The communications team will determine whether additional communication actions are required based on the type and volume of feedback or questions.	Will be ongoing at regular intervals within the program

Figure 19

4. Measure the communication or its performance. This process must tie directly back to your objectives for the communication program, and it will also probably tie in closely with the feedback process, which will be a primary source of measurement data.

The first draft of the objectives for Best Realty were not measurable. We've refined them now and included the key measures (see Figure 20 on page 142):

- Meet or exceed the legal requirements surrounding the communication of financial or employment-related information to employees. Key measures:

  ✠ Communicate the pension plan performance no later than 31 August.

✠ Communicate benefits costs increases no later than 30 September.

✠ Communicate business status and related lay-offs no later than 30 September.

● Communicate accurately and clearly to employees, and measure this based on feedback received. Key measures:

✠ Follow-up questioners should not exceed 10 percent of the population.

● Communicate realistically and set realistic expectations. Key measures:

✠ Include at least one message per communication that articulates the value that Best Realty places on its employees.

✠ Include at least one message per layoff communication that demonstrates how Best Realty supports the growth of employees and will help those employees being let go transition to the job market.

✠ Do not promise or imply that no more layoffs will be needed.

The Measurement Process			
#	Process Step	Description of Activity	Elapsed Time
1	Track that scheduling factors are met	This measure applies in particular to the communication of financial- and benefits-related information to employees.	N/A
2	Track feedback and questions	Jack will track how many employees submit questions to clarify messages in the communications. Questions seeking additional information will not be counted in this measure.	N/A
3	Message composition	Each communication will be reviewed to ensure it contains: 1. At least one message about the value Best Realty places in it employees. 2. At least one message about supporting the growth of employees. 3. At least one message about supporting the transition into the job market of laid-off employees. 4. No implication or promise that no more layoffs will be needed.	N/A
4	Measurement reporting	The comms team will monitor these measures and report back to Sue and Henry at monthly intervals regarding status.	1 business day

Figure 20

Corporate Storytelling

Refining the Communication Plan

At this point, our goal for the communication plan is to convert it to a detailed blueprint, or project plan, for completing the communications. In the preliminary plan, we had already incorporated audience and message details, as well as timing details based on the nature and needs of the project. In this chapter, we'll revisit the messages to ensure they are complete. We'll also break each communication down into a set of work activities based on the processes we defined. And by doing that, we'll also document a critical path and set of milestones for the communications.

From Communication Plan to Project Plan

If you're familiar with project planning software, such as Microsoft Project, you can use it to create your detailed communication plan. These programs do not usually have room to easily notate key message content for a communication. So, you will probably need to document that level of detail in a separate chart, similar to the one we used in the previous chapter.

If you'd rather not take a formal project planning approach to your communication plan, that's fine too! A simple spreadsheet can work perfectly, and it can also contain key message content, as well as tasks, dates, and resources.

The most important thing about a detailed plan is that it organizes the information you need into a usable, summary outline so that you and your teammates know what needs to be done when and by whom. The format or software that you use doesn't matter.

But don't shortchange yourself in trying to speed

things up. Be sure you ask all the questions you need to. Go over those *Who, What, When, Where* and *Why* questions, and put that information to work. Think through the list of communications, the proposed messages and media. Make sure everyone is clear on what they need to do — so that the communications have the effect and power your management team expects.

As you read over the detailed plan for Best Realty (Figure 21), note that a few things have changed from the preliminary plan. First, the pension plan report to employees is now going to happen after the company picnic rather than before. Also the all-hands meeting originally scheduled for mid-September has been rescheduled for the 20th of the month. Both these adjustments reflect the sort of fine-tuning that is expected to occur in the course of a project or communications program.

Other changes have to do with the content of the communications. Messages have been developed further and fleshed out. The schedule has been broken out according to the tasks that will have to be completed (see Figure 22 on page 146). Each task is clearly assigned, and the feedback and measurement steps are also included.

The current breakdown of tasks is grouped by specific communication, which doesn't give you or your teammates a linear view of all the actions that need to happen. This sort of view would also be possible with software such as Microsoft Project. However, you can approximate a linear view relatively easily with a spreadsheet by linking two areas in the same worksheet to provide a second, summary view of the tasks scheduled.

Detailed Plan

Item #	Deliverable	Audience	Key Message(s)	Media	Sender/spkr	Work Steps		
1	Company picnic reminder	All employees	Remind employees to set date aside and come for fun! Date Time Location Menu What to bring (family, sun block, etc.)	Memo hand-out and bulletin board posting	Sue and Henry	Draft comm Review w/ Sue & Henry Feedback rec'd Complete 2nd draft Review w/ Sue & Henry Finalize Make copies Distribute No feedback No measurement	Comms Sue/Henry Comms Comms Sue/Henry Comms Mary Mary N/A N/A	22 Jul 23 Jul 24 Jul 25 Jul 26 Jul 30 Jul 31 Jul 1 Aug
2	Company picnic	All employees and families	No business messages at all	Face-to-face	Sue and Henry	No activities	N/A	15 Aug
3	Pension plan memo	All fulltime employees	Report: Performance 1H of year Actions company is taking When employees will be advised of those changes Include info about: Who agent is Experience levels Past performance Agent contact info? Overview of pension plan or a pointer for more details, including Jack's name for feedback	Memo	Sue, as fund administrator; consider includ-ing fund agent name and con-tact info so people can contact him directly	Draft comm Review w/ Sue & Henry Feedback received Complete 2nd draft Review w/ Sue & Henry Finalize Make copies Distribute Track feedback: begin Feedback reports begin Monitor feedback for measurement criteria	Comms Sue/Henry Comms Comms Sue/Henry Comms Mary Mary Jack Jack Comms	2 Aug 5 Aug 7 Aug 8 Aug 9 Aug 13 Aug 14 Aug 16 Aug 16 Aug 23 Aug 23 Aug
4	Insurance rate increases announcement and handout	All fulltime employees	Tell new insurance costs and effective date(s) Report actions co. is taking to improve coverage options Include agent info as with pension plan memo, overview of health plan or a pointer for more details, and Jack's contact info	Make it part of the all-hands meeting for Sept. and issue a hand-out that peo-ple can take away	Henry, see if insurance agent can be present to answer ques-tions	Draft comm Review w/ Sue & Henry Feedback rec'd Complete 2nd draft Review w/ Sue & Henry Finalize Make copies Distribute Track feedback: begin Feedback reports begin Monitor feedback for measure-ment criteria	Comms Sue/Henry Comms Comms Sue/Henry Comms Mary Mary Jack Jack Comms	6 Sept 9 Sept 10 Sept 11 Sept 12 Sept 17 Sept 18 Sept 20 Sept 20 Sept 27 Sept 27 Sept
5	Pension plan status report and handout	All fulltime employees	Follow-up report on what the company has decided to do re: improving fund performance Include Jack's name for feedback	Make it part of the all-hands meeting for Sept. and issue a hand-out that peo-ple can take away	Sue, see if fund agent can be present to answer ques-tions	Draft comm Review w/ Sue & Henry Feedback rec'd Complete 2nd draft Review w/ Sue & Henry Finalize Make copies Distribute Track feedback: begin Feedback reports begin Monitor feedback for measurement criteria	Comms Sue/Henry Comms Comms Sue/Henry Comms Mary Mary Jack Jack Comms	6 Sept 9 Sept 10 Sept 11 Sept 12 Sept 17 Sept 18 Sept 20 Sept 20 Sept 27 Sept 27 Sept
6	Layoffs announcement	All fulltime employees	Explain that company will be making layoff decisions due to economic climate This is a difficult decision; people will be contacted directly no later than month-end Best Realty is committed to its employees: facts about opportunities for employ-ees to improve skills Best Realty will assist laid-off employees with 30 days of placement services OR $250 toward education.	Make it part of the all-hands meeting for Sept.; no handout	Sue and Henry	Draft comm Review w/ Sue & Henry Feedback rec'd Complete 2nd draft Review w/ Sue & Henry Finalize Make copies Distribute Track feedback: begin Feedback reports begin Monitor feedback for measurement criteria	Comms Sue/Henry Comms Comms Sue/Henry Comms Mary Mary Jack Jack Comms	6 Sept 9 Sept 10 Sept 11 Sept 12 Sept 17 Sept 18 Sept 20 Sept 20 Sept 27 Sept 27 Sept
7	Layoffs	Those being laid off	Confidential and personal dismissal with thanks and severance as per role in company Handout: Thank you and dismissal Handout: Contact information and instructions to obtain education or placement services	Face-to-face with escort to collect belong-ings and depart the premises; handout re: follow-up services being offered.	Sue or Henry	Draft comm Review w/ Sue & Henry Feedback rec'd Complete 2nd draft Review w/ Sue & Henry Finalize Make copies Distribute No feedback No measurement	Comms Sue/Henry Comms Comms Sue/Henry Comms Mary Mary N/A N/A	16 Sept 18 Sept 20 Sept 23 Sept 24 Sept 26 Sept 30 Sept 30 Sept N/A N/A

Figure 21

Fleshing Out the Plan

Detailed Plan Schedule		Company Picnic Reminder	Company Picnic	Pension Plan Memo	Insurance Rate Increases Announcement and Handout	Pension Plan Status Report and Handout	Layoffs Announcement	Layoffs
Comms	Draft comm	22 Jul	15 Aug	2 Aug	6 Sept	6 Sept	6 Sept	16 Sept
Sue/Henry	Review	23 Jul	N/A	5 Aug	9 Sept	9 Sept	9 Sept	18 Sept
Comms	Feedback rec'd	24 Jul	N/A	7 Aug	10 Sept	10 Sept	10 Sept	20 Sept
Comms	2nd draft	25 Jul	N/A	8 Aug	11 Sept	11 Sept	11 Sept	23 Sept
Sue/Henry	Review	26 Jul	N/A	9 Aug	12 Sept	12 Sept	12 Sept	24 Sept
Comms	Finalize	30 Jul	N/A	13 Aug	17 Sept	17 Sept	17 Sept	26 Sept
Mary	Make copies	31 Jul	N/A	14 Aug	18 Sept	18 Sept	18 Sept	30 Sept
Mary	Distribute	1 Aug	N/A	16 Aug	20 Sept	20 Sept	20 Sept	30 Sept
Jack	Track feedback: begin	N/A	N/A	16 Aug	20 Sept	20 Sept	20 Sept	N/A
Jack	Feedback reports begin	N/A	N/A	23 Aug	27 Sept	27 Sept	27 Sept	N/A
Comms	Monitor feedback for measurement	N/A	N/A	23 Aug	27 Sept	27 Sept	27 Sept	N/A

Figure 22

Defining Milestones and a Critical Path

Milestones are those events in a plan whose completion is critical. Once you define the milestones for a plan, taken together they make up the critical path. In large and complex projects, critical paths are very important to define because changes in timing along the critical path can affect many different work streams and quickly derail a project. In a smaller project, a team might not bother with this step. From a strictly communications point of view, I find this step useful to help me define what critical inputs I need to receive in order to meet my plan. Another term for this would be a *dependency*.

For example, to be able to complete the first deliverable in the plan for Best Realty, Mary would have to have finished arranging many of the logistics for the picnic so their details could be included in the reminder memo. If Mary does not complete these actions, then completion of the memo will be delayed.

While that example is relatively straightforward, there are others that are more complex — even in our Best Realty plan. The layoff handout requires specific information about the placement service and education options for laid-off employees. You must receive that information by September 23 to be able to include it in the final review with Sue and Henry. But suppose Jack, who is setting up that program, won't have the final details ironed out until later that week — on Thursday, September 26. You will have to adjust your schedule and possibly your delivery of the final communication to Mary for copying. Therefore, completion of the placement and education details is a milestone for this project overall.

It is a very good idea for you to spend some time with your detailed plan and make sure you are clear on what inputs from other members of the project are truly critical to your ability to complete your work. This will allow you to coordinate with other people more effectively. In a larger project, a project manager would do this coordination effort. In a smaller project, you will have to watch out for yourself.

Scenario 2: Fine Family Furniture

Where We Left Off

Just as with the Best Realty scenario, we accomplished a lot in the preceding chapter.

- Completed an audience analysis and outline of the

project, including key messages for the audiences.

● Identified the types of detailed information to include in the communications and who can provide that information for us.

● Identified the skills needed to produce the communications and people with those skills.

● Defined our communication objectives and guiding principles.

● Produced a preliminary plan detailing the proposed communications and their primary audience, media, and timing.

Where We're Headed Next

We closed the Fine Family Furniture section of the last chapter with a list of five sets of activities that we must complete. These activities reflect steps that will have to be added to or changed in the existing communication processes at Fine Family.

After we make these process adjustments for Fine Family Furniture, we'll return to the preliminary communications plan of the last chapter and work that into a detailed plan, complete with tasks, timelines, milestones, a critical path, and resources.

A Word About Process

Many mid-sized and large firms use business processes to run their companies. These are steps that employees follow to complete certain types of work activities. However, there are many other companies that don't rely on business processes to increase consistency and efficiency among employees. If this is the first time you've ever heard the term, don't worry.

The concept is actually very simple: to define a checklist that all employees can use to complete certain tasks in the company. Processes increase consistency and efficiency and thereby reduce costs, increase productivity, and improve quality.

For the purposes of our discussions here, we have assumed that Fine Family Furniture has an established communications process. We're not going to try to second-guess as to what that process is. Instead, we'll focus on the items that we know must be defined and agreed on for our plan to succeed. If we really did work for Fine Family Furniture, we would add these items to the existing process and remove those that aren't necessary for this project.

While this sounds like a lot of busywork, taking the time to do this has two advantages (in addition to the fact that you must do this in a process-managed company):

1. Processes provide clear instructions and expectations we can use with staff and teammates. This lets you delegate tasks more effectively and helps reduce the number of errors made by relying on memory and guesswork.

2. Processes are repeatable steps that can be reused at any time by anyone in the company, which gives us a foundation on which to act and also improve over time. It also makes it easier to hand over a communications package that can then be implemented in an entirely different part of the company.

What Processes Will We Define and Use?

1. Review the draft plan, objectives, and guiding principles with our manager, the VP, Human Resources, and the project's executive sponsor, the VP Finance (see Figure 23). This review step is a little bit different than the regular review cycle that we'll use for the development of the communications.

This review should confirm that management agrees with the plan's approach, goals, and tactics.

The Executive Review Cycle			(estimates)
#	Process step	Description of activity	Elapsed time
1	Draft plan, goals, guiding principles	Construct preliminary plan, goals, & guiding principles. Obtain input from audience experts & core project team.	Varies. 2 to 4 wks.
2	Review draft with VP Finance, VP HR, project manager (PM)	Distribute materials to execs for review. Conduct one-on-one or small-group meetings to review and discuss.	Varies. 1 week.
3	Receive comments	a. Consolidate all the feedback and review it. b. If there is conflicting feedback, review it with VP HR or PM to prioritize. c. If additional information is needed, get that information. d. If you don't know who has the information, ask PM for direction.	Varies. 1 to 2 wks.
4	Complete required revisions	Complete all modifications based on input received.	Varies. 3 to 5 days.
5	Review revised plan, goals, guiding principles	Same as step 2.	Varies. 3 to 5 days.
6	Receive comments/changes	Same as step 3.	Varies. 1 to 3 days
7	Finalize plan, goals, guiding principles	a. Comments on the revised plan should be minimal unless direction changes from sponsor. b. If there is still significant change, then you might need to create and circulate more drafts for review until feedback indicates acceptance.	Varies. 1 to 3 days unless further drafts and reviews are required.
8	Conduct quarterly reviews of plan, goals, guiding principles	Repeat steps 5-6. Will also want to include information about feedback and measurement to evaluate next steps.	Varies. 1 to 2 wks.
9	Complete required revisions and finalize	Repeat step 7.	Varies. 1 to 3 days.

Figure 23

These elements comprise the foundation on which all subsequent planning and action will be founded. Before we begin that more detailed work, we want to be sure that the people leading this project agree with what we propose to do.

Another person who should be included in this review is the project manager, who often works as the right-hand person to the project executive. It's important that he or she understands and agrees with the fundamentals underlying the employee communications activities.

We should plan on reporting back to these leaders at regular intervals, probably weekly, monthly, or quarterly, depending on the level of activity expected over the next 30 to 90 days.

2. Establish the review cycle and validate that process with our manager and the project executive. Every project is different. Does our executive want or need to be included in all content reviews? Or maybe just at the final review? Who else on the team needs to be included? Which communications will need to be translated into Spanish? All of them or just some?

In this type of project, we would expect that the core project team should review every communication and that every location should have the opportunity to translate the communications, so they must receive the content early enough to accomplish that. We'll assume, also, that the project executive wants to review the entire package and its components, but late in the development cycle when the core team is generally agreed upon the content and layout. The review cycle might look like Figure 24.

The Development Process and Review Cycle		(estimate)
# Process Step	Description of Activity	Elapsed Time
1 Draft communication	Construct the first draft of the communication, including graphic elements if available.	Varies. 1 week
2 Review draft with SMEs	Circulate the first draft for review by each SME in the review cycle. For Fine Family Furniture, this will be: a. Core project team members b. Audience or technical SME, depending on topic c. Distribution lead, for awareness	Varies. 1 business day for each
3 Receive comments	a. Consolidate all the feedback and review it. b. If there is conflicting feedback, review it with the PM to resolve. c. If additional information is needed, get it. d. If you don't know who has that information, ask the PM for direction.	Varies. 2 business days
4 Complete 2nd draft	Revise first draft based on feedback and direction rec'd.	2 business days
5 Review 2nd draft with SMEs	Same as step 2 but add the following: a. Company editor for style, grammar, and standards b. Project executive	1 business day
6 Receive comments & changes	Same as step 3.	2 business days
7 Finalize communication	a. Feedback and comments on 2nd draft should be minimal unless a direction change from the sponsor or information change from a subject matter expert. b. If changes are limited, then you should be able to do a final edit and release it as final to the distribution lead for packaging, possible translation and launch.	1 business day unless further drafts/reviews are required (see figure 23)
8 Translation	The distribution lead will coordinate all translation activities on behalf of local contacts.	5 business days
9 Packaging or printing	The distribution lead will coordinate all packaging and printing activities.	3 business days to 3 weeks

Figure 24

Many people have never acted as reviewers or subject matter experts in a communication program. Documenting these steps can be helpful to everybody to ensure they understand their part in the process. For example, reviewers should each get their comments back to you within no more than one business day, according to the process we've defined above. They should also know they need only give us their comments to correct or clarify content. They are not expected to rewrite the communication.

3. Define the distribution process and ensure HR resources are assigned to support it. This is a critical and often overlooked step. No matter how fantastically clear and accurate your communication might be, it's useless if it can't get to the people who need it. (See Figure 25.)

The Distribution Process			
#	Process Step	Description of Activity	Elapsed Time
1	Build communications distribution network	Establish contact with each retail and warehouse location to ensure a local communication contact is assigned for this project. Maintain a distribution list of these contacts. Communicate requirements for these contacts, such as developing and maintaining a distribution list for local workers according to segmentation requirements and arranging for all-hands meetings, bulletin board postings, and broadcast e-mails or other comms.	Ongoing
2	Coordinate translation	Translate individual comms for inclusion in the package or arrange for the translations to be done.	Allow 3-5 days to translate 2-3 pages of text
3	Serve as central distribution point for all project communications	Distribute e-mail and hard-copy communications packages to location comms leads for action locally.	Allow 3-5 days to review/compile pkg., another 7-10 days for mail distribution
4	Support the comms distribution network	Provide support to the local contacts to ensure they use the comms packages as planned. Be available to answer questions and assist further.	Ongoing
5	Track usage	Track compliance and use of the comms package.	Ongoing, incl. weekly status calls with network during peak periods
6	Monitor successes and challenges	Report back to project comms team regarding what worked in the package, what didn't work, and what would work better for the local retail and warehouse locations.	Ongoing, should incl. weekly or frequent reports during peak periods

Figure 25

For Fine Family Furniture, we established earlier that a member of the HR department usually fulfills the distribution function. Our responsibility is to request that person and provide them with the details they need to know to create and manage the right types of distribution lists and also to arrange for printing if posters, for example, are needed and for translation, when needed.

4. Work with the project manager to insert a communication test into the project plan. This activity should show up as a line or two on the project manager's overall project plan. It will then also show up as a deliverable on the communication plan.

The advantage of testing the communications as part of the functional testing of the new application and related education is that we will be able to get direct feedback about package elements in time to improve the messages and other components. Oftentimes, this step is left off, so take advantage of adding it whenever you can!

5. Define success criteria and how they will be measured. This set of steps must tie directly back to the program's objectives. It will also probably tie in closely with the feedback process, if there is one, which will be a primary source of measurement data.

The first draft of objectives for Fine Family were not measurable and had to be finetuned so that key measures could be included.

- Create a central communications package and components for use by all retail and warehouse locations that covers 95 percent of all messages for employees affected by the new system. Key measure:
  - ✠ Location modifications should total no more than 5 percent of the ultimate communications issued.

- Help drive 100 percent participation in the education activities to support the new system. Key measure:

  ⌘ Track enrollment numbers immediately before and after communication events to see if enrollment increases at least 50 percent as a result of a communication.

- Help drive 85 percent employee understanding, prior to deployment, of why this investment is being made and what is expected. Key measure:

  ⌘ Local communication contacts will monitor and report on perceived levels of employee understanding using existing all-hands meetings and team events to conduct observations. Do not institute any new employee or management team survey actions to obtain information.

The Measurement Process			
#	Process Step	Description of Activity	Elapsed Time
1	Track number and type of modifications to comms	Distribution lead will perform this activity and report weekly.	Ongoing
2	Track enrollment numbers	Communications team will work with education team to track enrollment numbers on a weekly or daily basis and then compare against communications schedule to determine impact. Report weekly on findings.	Ongoing
3	Track employee awareness	1. Distribution lead will support local communication contacts to track employee awareness at three all-hands meetings immediately prior to deployment. Observations need to be collected in specific areas as defined in a monitoring form that will be distributed with the communications package. 2. Distribution lead will report to communications and project teams weekly.	Ongoing

Figure 26

6. We didn't identify a feedback step in the pre-ceding chapter because the process Fine Family Furniture uses for employee communication always includes contact information for a resource to receive feedback or questions and then respond to employees. For this project, the distribution lead will also handle this responsibility.

Refining the Communication Plan

Okay, the next step is to convert the preliminary communication plan to a detailed blueprint, or project plan, for completing the communications. In the preliminary plan, we incorporated audience and message details, as well as timing details based on the nature and needs of the project. In this chapter, we'll revisit the messages to ensure they are complete and reconsider what elements need to be included in the package each location will use. We'll also break each communication down into a set of work activities based on the processes we defined. At that point we'll be able to document a critical path and set of milestones for the communications activities in the project.

From Communication Plan to Project Plan

Mid-sized and large companies often require project teams to use project-planning software, such as Microsoft Project. These programs do not usually have room to easily notate key message content for a communication. So, you also must document that level of detail in a separate chart, similar to the one we used in the preceding chapter.

If you'd rather not take a formal project planning

approach to your communications plan, that's fine. A simple spreadsheet can work perfectly, and it can also contain key message content, as well as tasks, dates, and resources.

The most important thing about a detailed plan is that it organizes the information you need into a usable, summary outline so that you and your teammates know what needs to be done when and by whom. The format or software that you use doesn't matter.

Above all, don't shortchange yourself in trying to speed things up. Ask all the questions you need to. Go over those *who, what, when, where,* and *why* questions and put the information to work. Think through the list of communications, the proposed messages and media. Make sure everyone is clear on what they need to do — so that the communications have the effect and power your management team expects.

In our example here (see Figure 27) we're sticking with a spreadsheet format. You'll notice that this detailed plan has two parts: a workflow part and a list of deliverables. The reason we've structured it that way is because our plan calls for a packaged communications approach in which the project team creates a set of communications to be issued at specific intervals. The local communications contacts will then insert specific details that their employees need to know, such as the date of education for their location and so on. The package contains placeholders for this information so that the local communications leads can easily see which details they're responsible to finalize and then insert into the e-mail or have printed up for use with the poster. The first portion of the detailed plan outlines the steps required to create the package and its components. The second part of the plan (see Figure 28) lists what those components are.

As with our Best Realty example, aspects of this plan have changed from the preliminary plan we created in the

Detailed Plan for Fine Family Furniture

#	Work Item	Owner	Description	Task
1	Draft package	Comms	Prepare drafts of all package components as described below.	Allow 2 weeks
2	Review package	Core project team, PM, Distribution lead, any other SMEs	Circulate package draft to all reviewers	Allow 1 week
3	Review feedback	Comms	Collect feedback from all reviewers and clarify any conflicting or incomplete feedback	Allow 1 week
4	Prepare 2nd draft	Comms, graphic designer	Revise package based on feedback	Allow 2 weeks
5	Review 2nd draft	Core project team, PM, Distribution lead, any other SMEs	Repeat step 2	Allow 3 days
6	Review feedback	Comms	Repeat step 3	Allow 3 days
7	Finalize package	Comms	Make final revisions to package based on second round of feedback	Allow 3 days
8	Test package	Comms with project team	Include communications in test scenarios	Allow 1 week
9	Revise package based on testing	Comms with project team	Monitor communications testing and compile observations and required changes	Allow 1 week
10	Final review	Core project team, PM, Distribution lead, VP Finance	This final review is mostly for information purposes and serves to alert the executive that the communications are final and ready to implement. Possibility exists for some last-minute changes.	Allow 3 days
11	Hand off for translation and final packaging	Comms to Distribution lead	Distribution lead obtains translation as needed; comms provides support if questions arise	Allow 1 week
12	Distribute to local contacts and begin weekly team calls to support use of package and help make req'd modifications	Distribution lead plus local contacts	Distribution lead distributes the package and coordinates use of it with local contacts; comms provides support if questions arise or changes are needed. If changes are significant, comms might have to reinitiate review cycles; however, most can be resolved without that.	Allow 1 day for e-mail and 7-10 days for hard-copy version

Figure 27

Detailed Plan for Fine Family Furniture

#	Launch Date	Deliverable	Audience	Message	Media	Sender
1	60 days prior to education	Cover letter for package	Location comms leads w/ cc's to store/facility mgrs	Announce beginning of communication activities State business objectives for project and position project in context of FFF's goals/culture Advise that detailed package contents will follow	E-mail	VP Finance
2	60 days prior to education	Package checklist	Location comms leads	Outline of package contents Instructions on how to use package & obtain support Information about weekly meetings during deployment periods for comms network Summary statement of recipients' roles and responsibilities	E-mail, hard-copy memo, suggested staff-directed memos and brochures (possible poster for lunchroom)	Distribution lead
3	30 days prior to education	Executive memo	All location employees	Announce education and deployment dates for location State req'd participation levels, time commitments, staffing and logistical requirements Contact info for more details Include brochure and general info for managers to reference	E-mail, hard-copy memo, suggested staff-directed memos and brochures (possible poster for lunchroom)	Location manager
4	30 days prior to education	Poster	All location employees	Visually brand the new system Remind employees to get ready to learn how to use the new system Portray happy customers and staff	Printed posters with pockets to hold location-specific info	Location manager
5	14 days prior to education	Action memo	All location employees	Confirm location's education and deployment schedules Reaffirm mandatory attendance at education and other expectations of employees Deliver prerequisite materials for self-study activities on employees' own time	Hard-copy memo with attached self-study, calendar, and checklist to confirm employee is ready	Location manager
6	3 days prior to education	Reminder memo	All location employees	Reminder of scheduled education and deployment activities, employee required actions, etc.	Hard-copy memo and possible signs for bulletin board	Location manager
7	3 days after productive use begins	Thank you memo and status report	All location employees	Thank employees for making the transition work well Report on how well the store did in terms of employee participation in training and deployment activities Will there be a contest and prize?	Issue hard-copy memo and bulletin board memo announcement; use in all-hands setting	Location manager
8	14 days after productive use begins	Interim status report	Senior executives and location managers	Report on early usage statistics Pinpoint any early user or behavior problems and related corrective action Transition location to be part of general monthly project status report beginning at month-end	E-mail and hard-copy version for use only by executives and location management	Location manager: last in project series

Figure 28

preceding chapter. That is to be expected. Plans are living documents and will constantly change as projects progress.

In a project like this, where we're going to create a package of communications for use by different locations with subtle audience differences, we need to remember that the package needs to be flexible to accommodate those subtle differences. We also need to allow for possible last-minute content changes if the project suffers a date setback or other change after the packages have been distributed or are even in use. The communication and distribution leaders will need to remain involved until all locations have completed the activities in the plan and communications deployment is complete. We might also want to create a contingency process in the event we have an urgent situation somewhere along the way. How, for example, will we get materials translated quickly enough if we have a last-minute change that affects when employees will learn to use the new system? Or what materials will not be translated if there are last-minute changes? Those sorts of parameters can be set in advance and save a lot of upheaval later on.

Defining Milestones and a Critical Path

As an employee in a mid-size or large company, you are probably aware that milestones are those events in a plan whose completion is critical. When taken together, milestones make up the critical path. In large and complex projects, critical paths are very important to define because changes in timing along the critical path can affect many different work streams and quickly derail a project. In a smaller project, a team might not bother with this step. From a strictly communications point of view, this step is useful in helping to define the critical inputs needed to meet the plan. Another term for this would be a *dependency*.

If a communication event is considered a milestone for the project, then we will need to work with the project manager to ensure the right communications details are included in the project plan. For example, perhaps education will not be possible unless the reminder communication happens exactly 14 days prior. This is a critical event for the project and should be noted on the project plan and on our communication plan.

An example of a communication milestone, and possibly also a project milestone, would be to exit testing within at least five days of beginning it. Otherwise, we won't be able to complete the revisions that might be needed before the package has to be submitted for translation. The translation date is also probably a milestone.

So, by completing our detailed communications plan we begin to define our milestones and critical path. This path is important so that other members of the project team understand how their activities impact other aspects of the project. Project managers should manage this type of project-level communication and coordination. But we have to be able to give him or her our requirements or else they will not be included. In addition, we could find ourselves without a piece of information or enough time to do what we have to do.

Well, that's it for this chapter! The next chapter should be a breeze because we've created great foundations for Best Realty and Fine Family Furniture. We've got detailed plans, clear objectives and guiding principles. We know who's supposed to do what, when. And we have a good understanding of our audience and our project and what people need to know or do.

If you're reading one scenario at a time, go ahead and move on. But do come back and read the scenario you first skipped so you catch any ideas mentioned that might be useful for your project and company.

The main activities we discussed here can be used in any internal communications project. They are

1. Know what you — or your predecessors — have accomplished so far, and then build on that work.

2. Decide what steps are needed next and define the processes needed — or modify the organization's existing processes to suit this project.

3. The processes a communications program usually includes are:

- Development and review cycles

- Distribution

- Measurement

- Feedback and continuous improvement

4. Refine the communications plan.

- Create a project plan, if desired.

- Or create a clear breakdown of tasks, timelines, and responsibilities.

5. With the detailed plan in hand, consider what the milestones and critical path are for your communications program.

Let's Do It! Execute the Plan

In the last chapter, we created a detailed communications plan, including measurable objectives and guiding principles, for two different scenarios: a small company with resource and benefits communications needs, and a larger company readying a new IT system.

In this chapter, we're going to put these plans to work. We won't prepare all the communications listed in each plan, but we will walk through at least one for each scenario. We'll also look at what has to happen to deploy or launch the communications. And we'll deal with feedback midstream that requires us to adjust our plan, our deliverables, and our messages.

As in the two preceding chapters, the smaller project comes first and the larger project follows. You can choose to read one at a time and skip the other one. Or you can read through both scenarios and then take what applies to your situation and modify it.

Scenario 1: Best Realty

Where We Left Off

We completed our planning work in the last chapter, so we are now ready to begin developing the communication items in that plan. It's important to remember that plans are only guidelines or blueprints. They don't cover absolutely every detail for a communications program, and they do change.

In projects that will run for some time, you should plan on returning to your plan at least quarterly to update and modify it to reflect changes that have taken place in the project over that period and that affect communications going forward.

For Best Realty, our communications program is relatively brief. We can expect to complete this plan and then move on to a new project.

In addition to the plan itself, completed in the last chapter, we also defined the processes that we'll use to develop, distribute, measure, and improve our communications. We will use these processes a lot in the activities covered in this chapter.

Where We're Headed Next

In this chapter, we're going to implement our plan. We don't have space in this book to create all the communications items in the Best Realty plan. But we will create at least one, and you might want to create others to practice your own development skills.

In addition to using our development process, defined in the preceding chapter, we'll also look at what has to happen to distribute the communication we develop. And we'll respond to new information midstream in the project. This new information will require us to modify our plan in some way, and we'll look at how to approach that type of situation.

The Fun Part — Creating the Deliverables!

Personally, I think this part is the best part of working in communications. This is where we sit down with our blueprint, the information from our subject matter experts, our understanding of the target audiences, our pen and paper or computer screen, and tell a story.

If it's a memo, it will be a short story. If it's a presentation or white paper, it will be longer. But our goal is to make it as interesting, as real and relevant, and as direct and succinct as possible.

Then we circulate that first draft for review according to the process we defined earlier.

Create, review, revise ... review, revise.

Let's take a crack at deliverable number 3 on the Best Realty plan: the pension plan memo. (See Figure 29.)

3	Pension plan memo	All full-time employees	Report performance 1H of year	Memo	Sue, as fund adminis-trator; consider including fund agent name and contact info so people can contact directly	Draft comm	Comms	2 Aug
						Review w/ Sue/Henry	Sue/Henry	5 Aug
			Report actions company is taking and when employees will be advised of any changes of decisions they must make			Feedback received	Comms	7 Aug
						Complete 2nd draft	Comms	8 Aug
						Review w/ Sue/Henry	Sue/Henry	9 Aug
			Include info about who agent is, experience levels, past performance			Finalize	Comms	13 Aug
						Make copies	Mary	14 Aug
			Include agent contact info?			Distribute	Mary	16 Aug
						Track feedback: begin	Jack	16 Aug
			Include overview of pension plan for employees or pointer to where they can get more details, include Jack's name for feedback			Feedback reports begin	Jack	23 Aug
						Monitor feedback for measurement criteria	Comms	23 Aug

Figure 29

Memo

16 August
Re: Employee Pension Fund 1H02 Performance

To all employees

Hello everybody! On 31 July, Target Accounts, the fund manager for the Best Realty employee pension fund, advised me as the fund administrator that the fund **decreased** in value by 18 percent during the period 1 January 2002 to 30 June 2002.

While this is not good news, it is also not as bad as it might sound. Let me put things into perspective for you.

> 1. Target Accounts has managed the Best Realty employee pension fund since its inception in 1997.

> 2. Annual performance since inception has average 8 percent gains in spite of two declines in 1999 and 2001 of 6 and 4 percent, respectively.

> 3. The decline in the first half of this year is consistent with market performance. The fund's performance is slightly above average when compared with that of other employee pension funds.

Target Accounts does not recommend any portfolio changes at this time. However, as fund administrator, I have asked our account manager at Target to conduct a more detailed analysis and report back to me with any findings and any recommended actions immediately after Labor Day. I will let you know the outcome of those conversations during the September all-hands meeting.

In the interim, those employees who are vested to any degree in the fund will receive a more detailed statement in the mail in the next few days.

If you have any questions about the information on that statement, contact Target's customer service representative. You are also welcome to schedule time with me to discuss our pension investments.

The Best Realty employee pension fund is a benefit provided by the company to employees who have worked full-time for Best Realty for a minimum of one year. Employees are vested in the fund yearly at 20 percent increments. Jack is available to answer questions about vesting increments and other employment benefits at Best Realty.

Sincerely,

Sue Best

Figure 30

This is going to be distributed as a hard-copy memo. It's from Sue, as fund administrator. Here's a possible first draft. (Figure 30.)

We now need to circulate it through the reviewers as laid out in the preceding chapter: Sue, Jack, the Target Accounts contact person, and Mary, Sue's secretary. And while that was the order we specified in the last chapter, we should consider reversing it so that we get Mary's perspective first, then confirm the data with the contact from Target and Jack, and then finally run it past Sue.

Word processors have built-in edit tracking capabilities, which can make the review and revision steps pretty easy. Here's how the draft might look after reviews (see Figure 31 on page 168) by Mary, Jack, and the person at Target Accounts.

Mary's input was to soften up the tone of the memo so that it sounded more like Sue, who is approachable, open, and plainspoken. The person at Target corrected some of the figures quoted in the memo, and Jack recommended moving the general bit about the pension fund to a different spot in the memo.

Given so many changes at this point — which isn't at all uncommon — we would be best served to make the changes and then send a clean copy to Sue to review. We could also note on that copy that Mary, Jack, and the Target account manager have reviewed this content. So, Sue would see a first draft that looks something like the letter on the page 169 (Figure 32).

You'll notice that we made some additional changes that weren't specified by any of the reviewers. That's great! With every iteration, take the time to consider what other organizational changes or wording tweaks might improve the communication just a bit more. In this case, a word — "the" — was missing from the first paragraph.

Depending on Sue's review and changes, we might

Memo

16 August
Re: Employee Pension Fund 1H02 Performance

To all employees

<u>Hello everybody!</u> On 31 July, Target Accounts, the fund manager for the Best Realty employee pension fund, advised me as the fund administrator that the fund **decreased** in value by 18 percent during the period 1 January 2002 to 30 June 2002.

<u>While this is not good news, it is also not as bad as it might sound. Let me put things into perspective for you.</u>

~~As required by law, I am informing you of this decline within thirty days.~~

~~The Best Realty employee pension fund is a benefit provided by the company to employees who have worked full-time for Best Realty for a minimum of one year. Employees are vested in the fund yearly at 20 percent increments.~~

Target Accounts has managed the Best Realty employee pension fund since its inception in 1997. Annual performance since inception has average 8 percent gains in spite of two declines in 1999 and 2001 of 6 and 4~~8~~ percent, respectively.

The decline in the first half of this year is consistent with market performance. <u>The fund's performance is slightly above</u> average when compared with <u>that of</u> other employee pension funds.

Target Accounts does not recommend any portfolio changes at this time. However, as fund administrator, I have asked <u>our account manager</u> at Target to conduct a more detailed analysis and report back <u>to me</u> with any findings and any recommended actions immediately after Labor Day. I will ~~report to~~ let you <u>know</u> ~~on~~ the outcome of those conversations during the September all-hands meeting.

In the interim, those employees who are vested to any degree in the fund will receive a more detailed statement in the mail in the next few days.

If you have any questions about the information on that statement, contact ~~the~~ <u>Target's</u> customer service representative ~~named on the statement~~. You are also welcome to schedule time with me to discuss our pension investments.

<u>The Best Realty employee pension fund is a benefit provided by the company to employees who have worked full-time for Best Realty for a minimum of one year. Employees are vested in the fund yearly at 20 percent increments.</u> Jack is available to answer questions about vesting increments and other employment benefits at Best Realty.

Figure 31

Memo

16 August
Re: Employee Pension Fund 1H02 Performance

To all employees

On 31 July, Target Accounts, the fund manager for the Best Realty employee pension fund, advised me as the fund administrator that the fund **decreased** in value by 18 percent during the period 1 January 2002 to 30 June 2002.

As required by law, I am informing you of this decline within thirty days.

The Best Realty employee pension fund is a benefit provided by the company to employees who have worked full-time for Best Realty for a minimum of one year. Employees are vested in the fund yearly at 20 percent increments.

Target Accounts has managed the Best Realty employee pension fund since its inception in 1997. Annual performance since inception has average 8 percent gains in spite of two declines in 1999 and 2001 of 6 and 8 percent, respectively.

The decline in the first half of this year is consistent with market performance and average when compared with other employee pension funds.

Target Accounts does not recommend any portfolio changes at this time. However, as fund administrator, I have asked Target to conduct a more detailed analysis and report back with any findings and any recommended actions immediately after Labor Day. I will report to you on the outcome of those conversations during the September all-hands meeting.

In the interim, those employees who are vested in any degree in the fund will receive a more detailed statement in the mail in the next few days.

If you have any questions about the information on that statement, contact the customer service representative named on the statement.

You are also welcome to schedule time with me to discuss our pension investments. Jack is available to answer questions about vesting increments and other employment benefits at Best Realty.

Sincerely,

Sue Best

Figure 32

need to circulate it to Mary, Jack, and Target one more time. But we might have a pretty final memo in hand, too. Every organization is different, and so is every executive or business owner. Some companies and people will agonize over every single word, over the placement of comma, and even the format of a date. Others will hardly even look at the thing, so you can't be sure that you've got the details right. Whichever tendencies your organization and management have, you'll be able to respond and accommodate their requests in a consistent and verifiable way. Stick to your processes and use your teammates and subject matter experts to ensure you get the facts straight.

Push the Button, Mail the Memo, or Run Those Copies!

In this example for Best Realty, we know that Mary is going to copy the final memo and then distribute it to employees in their mail cubbies. It's pretty straightforward because there are no dependencies or other things that have to be in line first. Once Sue is happy with the memo, it can be distributed. And Mary knows it's coming, so she's ready to do the copying and stuff those mailboxes.

Let's say, though, that there was a dependency — something else had to happen before this memo could be released. Maybe Jack had to officially log Sue's correspondence into a corporate record or ensure that Target Account received Sue's direction before this internal memo could be released to employees. We, or Mary, would have to ensure that these steps happened. In a small company, we could work it out among ourselves. In a larger company, that responsibility should be clarified. Probably Mary would take that to-do since our responsibility is to create the communication and hers is to distribute and coordinate that distribution with any other related activities.

Iteration, Reuse, and the Value of Repetition

We mentioned earlier that it takes more than one communication event to get a message across to recipients. When advertisers prepare campaigns, they structure repetition into the program to ensure that the target audience is touched by the key messages several times over a finite period of time. This technique improves the levels of recall and awareness that people have about a product or project.

Even in a small company, with a small communications program such as that for Best Realty, we can use the same techniques to our advantage.

First of all, the act of communicating is iterative; that means we do it over and over, with adjustments each time. And in a communication program in which we're focused on one or two main topics, we want to reuse messages and templates or other materials. By reusing messages in different formats or media, we reinforce the messages to the audiences and give people multiple opportunities to receive the information.

Also, people learn and receive information in different ways. Some people are visual learners. Others are aural. Still others retain information that they gain in hands-on activities or by doing. By including the same core messages in a memo, a conference or meeting, and a handout, we can get our messages across in multiple media and increase the likelihood that our employees have opportunities to receive the information in different ways. They can hear it, see it, and even touch it or employ it in a business situation.

In the memo that we just drafted we used two instances of reuse and repetition:

- We relayed information that most employees have probably received in other memos, meetings, or letters.

- The last paragraph about the pension fund and that it is one of the employment benefits provided by Best Realty is a message that employees have seen in other formats, such as the employee handbook.

It's critical in employee communications to set a clear context the readers can easily follow so that employees understand the connections between what might otherwise appear to be unrelated, isolated events. Employee morale will be higher in an environment where management seems to understand how the pieces fit together and affect staff as well as the overall business. It's our job as communicators to make sure those pieces of information are included — and that type of information also helps create the story effect. Collect the facts and relay them in a context that is meaningful to the recipients. We're back to our who, what, when, where, why!

Is It Working? How to Adjust Midstream and Keep It Fresh

As human beings, we tend to do what works — over and over again. Maybe it works from our point of view because it's easy and can be finished relatively quickly.

Maybe it works because employees have become accustomed to it and that seems enough. Maybe it works because we just haven't taken the time to consider other ways that might work better.

As human beings, we also eventually get bored with the same old stuff. So, even if we aren't forced to rethink our approaches because we receive feedback that points out a shortfall, we can and should put it on our list to revisit the basics of our program at regular intervals.

In Best Realty's program, Jack, Henry's assistant, is the person who collects all employee feedback as a result of the communications that we issue. Let's say that Jack gets a barrage of feedback after the pension plan memo is released. Employees have a lot of questions, and there are common themes to those questions from person to person. Rather than answer the same question ten or fifteen times, Jack recommends that Sue set up a short question and answer session one afternoon where everybody can get these questions answered in one fell swoop. Sue agrees, and Mary quickly gets a session set up for an afternoon only two business days after the memo was issued.

This is a change in the communication plan. Based on feedback from employees, Sue has added a whole separate communication event to the program. She will not need a handout, but she does need Mary to send out a short memo with the meeting information on it, which we can support her in doing. She also needs the Target Account manager to be present, and she needs someone to attend the meeting and take notes so that a follow-up memo can be drafted and sent to people who could not attend the question and answer session. That is a communication role that we would fulfill.

The other thing we can learn from this feedback is that employees, when they get bad news, often require face time with their direct supervisors or management. So while the memo was probably a good idea, in the future we would also plan on a follow-up question and answer session within a day or two of the memo being released. We will want to review our current plan and consider whether this type of change should be made at any other points.

That's It for Best Realty

This brings us to the end of the Best Realty scenario. If you'd like to practice your development skills, you could go ahead and create drafts of the other deliverables in our plan and then walk them through the review cycle and see where the process takes you.

If you have also been following the Fine Family Furniture scenario, then go ahead and read the rest of this chapter.

Scenario 2: Fine Family Furniture

Where We Left Off

In the last chapter, we created a detailed plan for Fine Family Furniture and identified the process steps, skills, and resources we'll use to implement the plan. Now we're ready to develop the communications and get the package drafted for testing.

Remember that plans are only guidelines, or blueprints. They don't cover absolutely every detail for a communication program, and they do change.

In projects that will run for some time, you should plan on returning to your plan at least quarterly to update and modify it to reflect changes that have taken place in the project over that period and that affect communications going forward.

For Fine Family Furniture, our approach is to create a package that can be reused from location to location throughout the duration of the IT implementation. Our goal is to test the package and then refine it before final distribution and use. Of course it's possible that even after testing we will come across content or components in the package that will need to be changed. So we will distribute the package only as locations need it rather than to all locations at once. That way we can control midstream changes a little more easily.

Where We're Headed Next

After all this planning and learning about audiences and topics, we're going to create the actual communications! We won't, in the book, create all the communications items, or deliverables, because we don't have time or space to do that. But we'll create at least one, and you can choose to create others simply to practice your own development skills.

We'll use our development process to create and finalize the sample communication. Then, we'll respond to new information midstream in the project. This new information will require us to modify our plan in some way, and we'll look at ways we can approach that type of situation.

The Fun Part — Creating the Deliverables!

Personally, this part of communications work is my favorite! This is where we sit down with our blueprint, the information from our subject matter experts, our understanding of the target audiences, our pen and paper or computer screen, and we tell a story.

If we're working on a memo, it'll be a short story. If we're drafting a presentation or white paper, it'll be longer. Whatever length or media, our goal is to convey information in an interesting, real and relevant, direct and succinct fashion.

Then we'll circulate our drafts for review according to the process we defined earlier.

Create, review, revise ... review, revise.

When developing a communications package, you need to think of developing each component individually and also as part of a sequence of communications. So, while the first task is to create each item, you must also create it in the context of the whole package and all the elements that will exist within it. The main effect of the package aspect is that you will be able to spread information out across the items in the package and build on messages that were delivered early in the package.

For our discussions here, we will draft most of the individual communications and circulate them once as a package. After that, we may find that some communications will be easier finalize than while others, so the reviews will diverge for a while. Eventually you will want to bring them all back together and circulate the entire package for review. You must step back and view the entire package for consistency, accuracy, completeness, and possible redundancy.

So let's take a crack at deliverables number 1 through 3 and 5 through 8. Deliverable number 4 is a poster with relatively little content. We can assume that we've given that to the graphic designer to work on while we work on these other elements. Here's how the first draft of the package might look.

#1 - Cover letter for package

To: Local communication contacts
Cc: Store and warehouse managers
Fr: VP Finance
Re: Welcome to the One Store project team!

Hello [name],

I am delighted to welcome you to our One Store project as a communication contact for your store or warehouse!

[Distribution lead' name] is leading the communication effort for the project team, and you will be working together to implement a standard communication package for all employees.

The One Store project is a critical initiative for Fine Family Furniture. I expect the company to realize considerable productivity improvements and also increased customer satisfaction and revenue. But we won't realize these improvements without a lot of hard work on everyone's part. Employees must learn to use a new computer system and new business processes. We have to change the ways we've done things in the past — and that takes concentration and time to do well.

Each location has been challenged to reach 100 percent participation in making this change — from attending classes to helping installation teams complete tasks over select weekends. Your ability to motivate fellow employees in [location name] is critical to our success!

[Distribution lead] will be contacting you shortly to review with you a communication package and other support mechanisms that will be available to you over the next three months.

I know you will approach this assignment professionally and with your usual expertise. I also hope you are as excited as I am about the opportunities this project holds for Fine Family Furniture and all of us who work here.

Best regards,
VP, Finance

#2 - Package checklist

To: Local communication contacts
Cc: Project communication lead
Fr: Distribution lead
Re: Your One Store communication package checklist is on the way!
Hello [name],

Welcome to the One Store project communication team! I look forward to working with you over the next several months.

You will be receiving this same information in hard-copy format within the next ten days. In the interim, please take the time to review the soft-copy elements contained here.

Our team meets weekly to review project status at each location. You should plan on joining this meeting beginning next Tuesday. The conference number 1-800-555-0987 with a passcode of 123434.

Our communication approach for this project incorporates a package that contains common messages for use by all locations. Placeholders are included in the package components for you to insert information that is unique to each location, such as dates for education and so forth.

The plan below will give you an overview of the package and its components. However, I would like to schedule a half-hour conversation with you to answer any questions you might have so that you are fully prepared for the group meeting next Tuesday. Please let me know when would be a good time for within the next two to three days.

Thank you!
Distribution lead

[Attachment: summary plan and statement of roles and responsibilities]

#3 - Executive memo for use in each location

To: All location employees
Cc: Location One Store project team
Fr: Location manager
Re: Announcing the One Store project!

Hello,

The One Store project is a critical initiative for Fine Family Furniture that will make us more productive and more successful!

The project will install a single computerized system in our store/warehouse — and every other Fine Family Furniture location — to make it possible to manage our inventory and conduct credit checks in real-time.

It's going to take some work on our part, and I want to give you an idea now of what will be expected of all of us over the next several months.

First, [name and name] are leading the installation here in [location]. Their team includes [insert names of critical team members and their responsibilities]:

Second, every single one of us will be expected to learn to use this new application. Exact dates for the required education will be given to you within the next 30 days.

Third, all of us will also be expected to help the installation teams during the two weekends they will be here to actually hook up the system. Your supervisors will circulate a sign-up sheet for these activities within the next 30 days.

And finally, we all have to make a conscious choice to do things differently — in a new way that allows us to be part of a larger, broader, and more effective company than ever before. With this new technology, we'll be able to communicate more quickly and accurately among stores and warehouses. We'll be able to answer customers' questions more quickly. But we'll also have to learn how to work *together to do these things well and with continued respect for each other, our business, and our customers.*

It will be a challenge as the new technology is installed and we're trained — and still expected to meet our business goals. But I believe our team can do this and do it well! And I believe the advantages we'll gain individually and as an organization will make the investment of time and energy more than worthwhile!

So, I ask for more than your cooperation. I ask for your active support and commitment to bringing Fine Family Furniture into the 21st century.

Best regards,
Location manager

[Attachment: brochure]

#5 - Action memo for use in each location

To: All location employees
Cc: Location One Store project team
Fr: Location manager
Re: One Store education and installation schedule

Hello,

I want to confirm that education for the One Store installation will begin [date]. Please see your supervisor to enroll for a session if you have not already done so.

Installation will take place [date]. You must participate for at least two hours each weekend. Please see your supervisor to sign up for an activity if you have not already done so.

There are two self-study activities you must complete prior to attending the education sessions. That material is attached to this memo. Please download it and complete it at home. Contact [name] if you have any questions about this assignment. The study effort should take you no more than three hours.

Best regards,
Location manager

[Attachment: self-study module]

#6 ~ Reminder memo for use in each location

To: Select location employees [who have not completed required education and installation enrollment activities]
Cc: Location One Store project team
Fr: Location manager
Re: One Store education and installation URGENT REMINDER

Hello,

This is a reminder that you must enroll for an education session for the new One Store system, and you must attend that session. You must also complete the prerequisite self-study course before attending your session.
Employees who have not completed all these actions by [date] will be removed from the work schedule until the actions are complete.
You must also sign up for and participate in an installation activity on each of the two installation weekends.
I realize this is a lot of extra work at a very busy time of the year. Unfortunately, we have no alternative. The installation of our One Store system is only one event in a complex series of events that are coordinated across our

entire company. Each employee and each location is being impacted in the same way — and each employee and location is also being offered huge opportunities to improve their skills and chances to succeed.

If you haven't already, take the time now to complete the actions that are required to improve your company's effectiveness and your own ability to satisfy customers.

> *Best regards,*
> *Location manager*

[Attachment: self-study module]

#7 - Thank you memo and status report for use in each location

To: All location employees
Cc: Location One Store project team
Fr: Location manager
Re: Thank you and congratulations!

Hello team!

I am delighted to tell you that the One Store system is up and operational for our location! Well done!

This is a TREMENDOUS ACHIEVEMENT on everybody's part. The project team did an excellent job of coordinating the many events that had to take place.

Every employee here delivered in terms of commitment and enthusiasm — you completed all the required education and installation activities at XXX percent!

I am very proud of all of us! And over the next several months, as we grow accustomed to the new system, I am confident that we will each individually and also collectively realize the benefits we expect: more productivity, more customer satisfaction, and more revenue!

Best regards,
Location manager

#8 ~ Interim status report for use in each location

To: All location employees
Cc: Location One Store project team
Fr: Location manager
Re: One Store status report

Hello team!

It's good news! Early usage statistics show that we are making excellent/good/fair use of the new One Store system.

More than XX percent of you use the system at least once per day.

More than XX percent of you assist customers in making direct inventory or credit inquiries using One Store.

Calls for support assistance have decreased by XX percent since installation — only XX days ago.

And closed sales have increased A) back to our pre-installation average/high [or] B) XX percent over our pre-installation average/high for this time of year.

I continue to be very proud of the high levels of professionalism that have been displayed throughout this challenging process.

This will be the final memo to you about the One Store project. Our project team will issue subsequent status reports directly to the central project team and leadership every two weeks.

If you would like updates on how the project is progressing across the company, please see your supervisor. They will be able to give you summary updates or direct you to a better, central resource.

And again, thanks to each of you for your continuing hard work!

Best regards,
Location manager

A Few Comments About the Specifics

Note that the plan calls for all these memos to be delivered in e-mail format with parallel delivery in hard-copy format. Fine Family Furniture uses a simple e-mail program, so there's no formatting to do. All the hard-copy versions of the e-mails will be on a standard company memo template, so it's just a matter of moving the final content into the template.

The attachments offer some opportunities for enhanced graphics, but even those need to be relatively simple so that local printers can output the attachments. If locations want to formally print them up, they have that option. But our assumption is that they will not want to spend money to print the brochure but rather simply output it in black and white on a location printer.

In any case, our first pass at these communications focuses on the content more than on the formatting that might be used to deliver it. This sort of development approach requires reviewers to use their imaginations to visualize how the content will ultimately look when put into the company's memo format, etc. Some people have better visualization skills than others, so it's reasonable to expect some confused feedback during the review process because the graphical aspects are not included in the drafts.

We now need to circulate it through the reviewers as

laid out in the preceding chapter: the core project team, audience and topic experts, and the distribution leader.

We can expect the review process to last several days, at minimum, and to run through several iterations of the package and its components. Our process in the last chapter asked reviewers to respond with comments in only one day. Given the package review approach, we might want to adjust that to be more like three to five business days for review and comment.

Once the components have reached some stability, we will want to clean up the drafts and take the package to our manager and the VP Finance. The distribution lead should also be part of that review in case distribution-related questions arise.

At each iteration we should take the time to consider what other organizational changes or wording tweaks might improve the communications just a bit more. Every organization is different, and so is every executive. Some companies and people will agonize over every single word and even just the placement of comma. Others will hardly even look at the thing, so it's hard to be sure that we've got the details right. Whichever tendencies your organization and management have, you'll be able to respond and accommodate their requests in a consistent and verifiable way by sticking to your processes and using your teammates and other subject matter experts to ensure you get the facts straight.

Push the Button, Mail the Memo, or Run Those Copies!

For Fine Family Furniture, the distribution lead in the HR department is going to coordinate deployment of the packages and then also of the components of those packages within each location. Other situations will be very different, requiring very different approaches to distribution. These distribution variables can and will affect development. That reminder goes right back to our earlier work. If you target messages, for example, to a level of detail that the distribution capabilities in a company can't support, you're doing extra work for no good purpose. On the other hand, if you just compile a lot of general information and then send it to highly segmented distribution lists, you haven't addressed the unique information needs of those segments adequately. You must balance the development activities with the distribution realities and capabilities.

You also have to ensure that the sequence of communication events happens correctly. This is a big part of the distribution lead's job for Fine Family Furniture. He or she must ensure that the locations understand how to use the package of communications and then sequence those communications correctly. For example, the memo from the VP, Finance must go out before the memo from the distribution lead. It sounds obvious, but these are examples of the types of little details that can mess things up if missed.

Iteration, Reuse, and the Value of Repetition

We mentioned earlier that it takes more than one communications event to get a message across to recipients. When advertisers prepare campaigns, they structure repetition into the program to ensure that the target audience is touched by the key messages several times over a finite period of time. This technique improves the levels of recall and awareness that people have about a product or project.

Even in a mid-sized company, with a relatively small communications program such as that for Fine Family Furniture, we can use the same techniques to our advantage. And we have — these concepts are built into the package approach of our plan.

First of all, the act of communicating is iterative — that means we do it over and over, with adjustments each time. And in a communication program in which we're focused on one or two main topics, we want to reuse messages and templates or other materials. By reusing messages in different formats or media, we reinforce the messages to the audiences and give people multiple opportunities to receive the information.

Also, people learn and receive information in different ways. Some people are visual learners. Others are aural. Still others retain information that they gain in hands-on activities or by doing. By including essentially the same messages in a memo, a conference or meeting, and a handout, we can get our messages across in multiple media and increase the likelihood that our employees, who are all different, have different ways to receive the information. They can hear it, see it, and even touch it or employ it in a business situation.

In the draft package we employed several instances of reuse and repetition:

- Benefits statements across the several memos are similar.

- Expectations are similar and reinforced.

It's critical in employee communications to set a clear context that employees can easily understand. This way seemingly unrelated and isolated events will take their places in the larger, intentional scheme of things. Employee morale will be higher in an environment where management seems to understand how the pieces fit together and affect staff as well as the business, overall. It's our job as communicators to make sure those pieces of information are included — and that type of information also helps create the story effect. Collect the facts and relay them in a context that is meaningful to the recipients. We're back to our *who, what, when, where, why*!

Is It Working? How to Adjust Midstream and Keep It Fresh

As human beings, we tend to do what works — over and over again. Maybe it works from our point of view because it's easy and can be finished relatively quickly. Maybe it works because employees have become accustomed to it and that seems enough. Maybe it works because we just haven't taken the time to consider other ways that might work better.

As human beings, we also eventually get bored with the same old stuff. So, even if we aren't forced to rethink our approaches because we receive feedback that points out a shortfall, we can and should put it on our list to revisit the basics of our program at regular intervals.

In Fine Family Furniture's program, the distribution lead monitors feedback and measurement aspects of the program. Let's say that this person gets a barrage of feedback after the package is used at two locations. Supervisors complain that the tone of the action and reminder memos is too curt and that some employees, particularly those who speak Spanish, feel insulted. This factor then makes it very difficult to motivate employees to enroll for education, complete the prerequisites, and sign up for installation activities.

The project team agrees that these communications must be modified immediately. The third location is just entering the communication phase of the project; so all changes must be completed within two business days to allow them to translate the memos.

This is a change in the communications plan. While no new communications have been added, the team has to make a quick adjustment to effect the change without slowing the overall deployment schedule. And the change must then be incorporated in all remaining packages. Some of those might have been distributed already, and we'll have to attend to the details to ensure the most current versions of these memos get used going forward.

That's it for Fine Family Furniture, This Chapter and The Book

This brings us to the end of the Fine Family Furniture scenario. If you'd like to practice your development skills, you could go ahead and create second and third drafts of the package.

Index of General Charts, Forms and Matrices

Order another title
from the ABCs of Business series!

A Public Relations Survival Kit
by S. E. Slack   ISBN 0-9714988-0-6 $24.95   176 pp.

Discover the truth about public relations - that it's easy, it's logical and it doesn't have to cost half your budget. Slack takes on the myth that smaller businesses can't handle public relations without help and delivers this knock-out punch: Public relations is not rocket science. PR consultants just want you to think it is.

Order from your local bookstore or by visiting the Grendel Press Web site at http://www.grendelpress.com. Or take advantage of the special offer below!

SPECIAL MAIL ORDER OFFER: 25% OFF WITH THIS FORM

NAME: _____

ADDRESS: _____

CITY, ST & ZIP _____

PHONE: _____

My check is enclosed ____   VISA/MC/Discover ____
                                    (All areas of this form must be completed to
                                    process credit cards)
                                    Card number: _____

Quantity:___ @ $18.71=_____   Expiration date: _____   (mm/yyyy)

3.7% Tax: _____   Name as it appears on card:
(CO residents only)

S&H: $4.95   _____   **Mail to:**
(add $1.35 for each addt'l book)   Grendel Press
                                    ATTN: Special Orders Dept.
Total: _____   Offer: PRKIT200202
                                    P.O. Box 238
Photocopies of this form will be accepted.   Loveland, CO 80539-0238
Source Code: CSTOR200201